KESHER

A Journal of Messianic Judaism

ISSUE 23 / FALL 2009

SUBSCRIPTIONS

Online:

1-year subscription (2 issues) @ $18 and complete access
to all archived issues

Print:

2-year subscription (4 issues) @ $28 or
5-year subscription (10 issues) @ $65

Multiple Copy Print:

5 copies of 2-year subscription (4 issues) @ $120 or
5-year subscription (10 issues) @ $275 —
10 copies of 2-year subscription (4 issues) @ $240 or
5-year subscription (10 issues) @ $575

To place a subscription go to www.kesherjournal.com.

©2009 by MJTI Publications
ISBN: 978-1-60608-994-1
Published jointly by Wipf and Stock, 2009

KESHER

A Journal of Messianic Judaism

Andrew Sparks, M.Div., S.T.M., M.B.A.
EDITOR-IN-CHIEF

Elliot Klayman, J.D., L.L.M., M.A.
ASSISTANT EDITOR

Deborah Pardo-Kaplan, M.A., M.Sc.
ASSISTANT EDITOR

Jonathan Kaplan, M.Div., M.A., A.M.
ASSISTANT EDITOR

David Rudolph, Ph.D.
ASSISTANT EDITOR

ADVISORY BOARD
Rabbi Stuart Dauermann
Rabbi Barney Kasdan
Rabbi Richard Nichol
Rabbi Russell Resnik
Rabbi Paul Saal

Table of Contents

Issue 23 – Fall 2009

Dear Friend,

I am excited to share about some new developments with *Kesher: A Journal of Messianic Judaism.*

First of all, *Kesher* has now joined with the Messianic Jewish Theological Institute (MJTI). The partnership of a journal with a premier institution of Messianic Jewish learning is a great match. In addition to the contribution of leaders throughout the Messianic Jewish community, MJTI scholars and students will contribute to the journal. The back cover of this issue provides an overview of MJTI's misson to teach and live a vision of Jewish life renewed through Yeshua.

You can continue to access *Kesher* online at www.KesherJournal.com, where there are now additional offerings as *Kesher* is now part of the MJTI Network of websites. For those of you who have not yet subscribed online, you can access a selection of free online *Kesher* articles.

Please show your support by subscribing, renewing a subscription, or donating toward placing the journal in the hands of those who are not able to subscribe. *Kesher* sends out hundreds of copies to this end and provides free subscriptions to students engaged in Messianic Jewish learning.

In Messiah's service,

Andrew Sparks

Andrew Sparks, Editor-in-Chief

Andrew has served the Messianic Jewish community for more than fifteen years. Currently, he serves as Chief Advancement and Operating Officer of the Messianic Jewish Theological Institute. He holds an M.Div. (Westminster Theological Seminary), S.T.M. (Yale University), and M.B.A. (Fox School of Business, Temple University).

Hesed and Hospitality:
Embracing Our Place on the Margins

RUSSELL RESNIK

On a recent Shabbat morning, after the Torah reading, the rabbi opened his d'rash by saying:

> Judaism is a religion of law. In Judaism, we ask the question, 'What does the halacha say I should do?' Christianity is different. It likes to ask, 'What would Jesus do?' But we already know what Jesus would do—he would keep the halacha!

We Jews, the rabbi seemed to say, understand Jesus better than do his Christian followers. Jesus is one of us and would live accordingly. Thus, the rabbi managed in one stroke to both reclaim Yeshua as a great Jewish figure and to marginalize him and his adherents. He was following a long tradition among American Jewish leaders who "extracted Jesus from his Christian milieu, relocating him inside their own religious world, and then drawing on his cultural authority to criticize the very Christians whose favor they were supposedly currying."[1] Unlike the Christians, the rabbi's Jesus would certainly not expect his fellow Jews to "get saved" or to acknowledge him as the divine Messiah. Indeed, this Jesus is just trying to be a good Jew and does not belong at the center of anyone's story.

The rabbi's words reminded me of the scene in Yeshua's home synagogue in Nazareth, where he rises to read the announcement of the eschatological jubilee in the scroll of Isaiah. When he returns to his place among the congregants, he declares, "Today this Scripture is fulfilled in your hearing" (Luke 4:14–21). The congregation seems impressed with Yeshua's words at first, but ends up asking, "Who does he think he is anyway?" Yeshua's marginalization in this episode is quite literal; he is driven outside of town to the brow of the hill on which it is built, where he barely avoids being thrown down the cliff.

---

1. Stephen Prothero, *American Jesus: How the Son of God Became a National Icon* (New York: Farrar, Straus and Giroux, 2003), 251.

Yeshua is indeed "The Misunderstood Jew," as described in a recent title by Amy-Jill Levine, Professor of New Testament Studies at Vanderbilt University.[2] Levine and the rabbi both imply that Yeshua is misunderstood first by his own followers, including, in Levine's view, the writers of the New Testament, who already began to rework Yeshua's Jewish message into something that would appeal to the growing contingent of Gentile followers. We can trust in the reliability of the apostolic writings, however, and still recognize Yeshua as a misunderstood and marginalized figure. In the words of John P. Meier, he is "a marginal Jew from a marginal province at the eastern end of the Roman Empire [who] left no writings of his own . . . no archaeological monuments or artifacts . . . nothing that comes directly from him without mediators."[3] This sort of marginality complicates the quest for the historical Jesus in which Meier's multi-volume series, *A Marginal Jew*, is engaged, but is only part of the story. The title of the series is also "intended to signify such things as Jesus' insignificance and socially marginal position in his own time as an itinerant prophet executed by the state, as well as Jesus' dissonance with teachings and practices more characteristic of Jewish religion of his time."[4]

This picture of Yeshua's marginality is consistent with the Gospel accounts. What is more striking there, however, is Yeshua's embrace of the margins to reveal the God who is at the center of Israel's story. In a culture infected with materialism and self-absorption, the margins are a prophetic location where one can protest yet not disappear. Yeshua's example beckons us to the margins as well. Perhaps it is fitting that the Messianic Jewish community, which sees itself at the center of God's redemptive purposes for both the church and the Jewish community, finds itself marginalized by both.

This paper considers both the inherent marginality of following a cross-bearing Messiah, and the incidental marginality that has resulted from the historic rift between the Jewish Messiah and the Jewish people, and between Jews and Christians. Inherent marginality is part of loyalty to Yeshua. Incidental marginality may change with time and circumstance, and the boundary between incidental and inherent marginality is often not clear. I conclude that we are to embrace marginality, even as

2. Amy-Jill Levine, *The Misunderstood Jew: The Church and the Scandal of the Jewish Jesus* (New York: HarperSanFrancisco, 2006).

3. John P. Meier, *A Marginal Jew: Rethinking the Historical Jesus. Volume One: The Roots of the Problem and the Person* (New York: Doubleday, 1991), 25.

4. Book review, Larry W. Hurtado, *Journal of Biblical Literature*, Vol. 112, No. 3 (Autumn, 1993): 532–34.

we seek to reverse our incidental marginality within Israel. We embrace marginality, whether inherent or incidental, as a platform for the practice of *hesed*, deeds of loving-kindness, including hospitality as a communal expression of *hesed*. Such expressions of *hesed* directly counter dominant cultural values to display the character of the Messiah whom we profess to follow.

Messiah on the margins

Before we embrace our place on the margins, however, we need to consider how Yeshua embraced his. Levine interprets the story of the woman at the well in her chapter on "Stereotyping Judaism." The story has been read by feminists as an example of Yeshua's reaching out to women, even outsider women, in a radically new way. So far so good, but such interpreters, as Levine points out, have often gone on to portray Yeshua as defying the whole allegedly oppressive, misogynist system of Judaism in order to bring hope to women. Levine suggests that in the story itself, "it is Jesus, the Jew in the Samaritan area, who is the 'outsider,' who behaves in a shameless way, and who is marginal to the community."[5] Time will not permit a response to Levine's claim that Yeshua was behaving in a shameless way, by exchanging suggestive banter with this flirtatious female stranger. Nor can I agree with Levine's claim that the woman is not an outsider in the story.[6] But Levine's central point, that Yeshua comes as an outsider and willingly inhabits the margin in this encounter, is well taken.

The woman at the well, of course, reminds us of a series of similar encounters in the Torah, as Levine notes.[7] First, in Genesis 24, Abraham sends his unnamed servant back to the ancestral homeland to find a bride for Isaac. The servant arrives at the outskirts of Nahor in the evening, and pauses at the well. He prays that the young woman who responds to his request for a drink by offering to water his camels as well will be the one the Lord has chosen, and so it comes to pass. The servant, and through him Isaac, is a marginal figure in this setting, an outsider subject to the kindness of the insiders. But he is a well-stocked outsider, with a whole caravan of gifts to bestow.

Isaac's son Jacob returns to the same land and comes upon a well (Gen 29), as a far more marginalized figure than his father. Unlike Isaac, he has no proxy, but must

5. Levine, 135.

6. Ibid.

7. Ibid., 137.

make the long journey himself. Indeed, he arrives at the well because he is fleeing for his life from the wrath of Esau, and he arrives empty-handed. Isaac, through the servant, can offer abundant gifts as a bride price. Jacob has only his own body and labor to offer. But his descendant Moses, in the third well-encounter in Torah (Ex 2) is even more marginalized. Like Jacob, he is fleeing for his life from the wrath of a powerful figure, and he arrives empty-handed. Jacob, however, has at least returned to the homeland of his mother's family; Moses does not return to any ancestral homeland. Indeed, even after he reveals himself as a hero and marries his bride, he declares, "I have been a stranger in a strange land" (Exod 2:22, AV).

The trajectory is clear: the outsider who arrives at the well becomes more and more marginal in each successive story. In all three stories, however, the outsider reveals himself as a heroic figure as well. At the well, Isaac's servant shows a hint of his riches to Rebecca (Gen 24:22). At the well, Jacob rolls away a massive stone to enable Rachel to water her flocks (Gen 29:10). At the well, Moses stands up to defend the seven daughters of Reuel the priest, including Zipporah his bride-to-be, against the abusive shepherds (Exod 2:17). And in each story, after this initial revelation at the well, the protagonist meets the family and wins his bride.

Yeshua enters this ongoing story by coming to Samaria as an outsider. Just as the Jews marginalized Samaritans, so did Samaritans marginalize Jews,[8] as the Samaritan woman points out in what seems to be a mocking tone: "How is it that You, being a Jew, ask a drink from me, a Samaritan woman?" (John 4:9). Traditional commentaries tend to miss Yeshua's marginality here and focus on that of the woman. Thus, Raymond Brown summarizes the exchange:

> Vs. 7. *Jesus* asks the Samaritan for water, violating the social customs of the time.
>
> Vs. 8. *Woman* mocks Jesus for being so in need that he does not observe the proprieties.
>
> Vs. 9. *Jesus* shows that the real reason for his action is not his inferiority or need, but his superior status.[9]

True, Yeshua does reveal his "superior status" in a sense, just as Abraham's servant, Jacob, and Moses reveal their superior status through heroic deeds at the well. Like

---

8. Ibid., 36.

9. Raymond E. Brown, "The Gospel according to John I-XII" in *The Anchor Bible* (New York: Doubleday, 1966), 177. Brown gives only passing reference to the connection with the well encounters in the Torah (Ibid., 170).

his ancestors, Yeshua performs a heroic deed there, in his case by offering living water to the woman. Like the servant of Abraham, Yeshua bears abundant gifts, speaking of the "gift of God" that he has to offer (John 4:10). He then shows his supernatural insight into the woman's personal life. But the outcome is more nuanced than Brown suggests; it is precisely within his perceived marginality and need that Yeshua is able to reach this woman. When he asks her to return with her husband, it is not merely to "uncover her evil deeds,"[10] as Brown says, nor to remind her "of her many disappointments in personal relationships in order that she may appreciate the more deep and lasting satisfaction that Jesus brings,"[11] as F.F. Bruce more kindly suggests. Rather, Yeshua continues to follow the pattern set in Torah in which each hero, after encountering the woman at the well, must meet the folks.

It is impossible to overlook the contrast between the Samaritan woman with five ex-husbands and a current paramour, and the beautiful Rebecca whom the text describes as "a virgin; no man had known her" (Gen 24:16). Within her questionable situation, however, the Samaritan woman ends up introducing Yeshua not just to her family, but to the entire city. Like the servant of Isaac, Yeshua has abundant gifts to offer. Unlike him, he gains not one bride, but a multitude of Samaritans.

It is no accident that in John's narrative the fruitful encounter with the Samaritan woman comes right after the more ambiguous encounter with a Jewish man in chapter 3. There too, Yeshua is a marginal figure, approachable only at night, but the non-marginal Nicodemus seems unable to embrace him as such. As Levine points out, "The unnamed Samaritan woman understands Jesus, while Nicodemus, the elite teacher, fails to get the point, and the unexpected result provides satisfaction to those outside the academy and the institutional church,"[12] a category that would include much of our Messianic Jewish constituency.

On the Jewish margins

Yeshua is in no hurry to reveal his "superior status." Rather, he willingly inhabits the margins to reveal his true identity. This strategy has particular relevance today, if we understand marginalization as an extreme form of our modern disease of hyper-individualism and the social fragmentation that it carries. In more traditional cultures, those on the margins are doomed to a sort of imposed hyper-individualism

10. Ibid., 177.

11. F.F. Bruce, *The Gospel of John.* (Grand Rapids, MI: Eerdmans, 1983), 107.

12. Levine, 138.

that leaves them isolated from the community. Today, we can see the marginalized as those for whom individualism has gone amok, those who must live among the ruins of the social fragmentation that affects us all in more subtle ways. Yeshua takes on this marginalization, embraces it, most completely in his cross, and there reconciles us with God. Yet, even though our marginalization from God has been overcome, in following Yeshua, we often find ourselves on the margins of our culture.

In the context of Jewish history, this irony is most pronounced. Aligning with Yeshua, at least outwardly, was a way for Jews in Christendom to escape the margins and move toward the mainstream of Gentile culture, which is precisely why we Messianic Jews are suspect to the Jewish community today. Only in recent decades has the social advantage of loyalty to Yeshua disappeared, and we can understand why the Jewish community remains suspicious of us. Confessing faith in Yeshua was once a key to escaping the margins of the wider Christian culture. We all remember the story of the Jewish convert who is a professor in Tsarist Russia. He is asked if he converted out of conviction, or for convenience. "Out of conviction," he replies. "The conviction that I'd rather be a professor at the St. Petersburg academy than teach the *yeshiva boochers* in my home *shtetl.*" Today, at least in the West, such compromise is unnecessary, but faith in Yeshua remains suspect, and therefore marginal within the Jewish community. This is an incidental marginality, shaped by history and culture, rather than the marginality inherent to the gospel. Nevertheless, the margins may be a prime position from which to express something of the reality of the Messiah whom we profess to follow.

I opened with a reference to a *d'rash* that I heard at a local synagogue I occasionally visit. The doors of this synagogue would normally be wide open to a nicely dressed Jewish man who seems to know his way around the service. After I had attended a few services, however, I felt that as a Messianic Jewish leader I needed to let the rabbi know who I was and even to gain his approval for my continued attendance, which I did via email. The rabbi responded graciously, but still seems a bit nervous whenever I attend. At one point in our correspondence he said:

> Christianity defines who is a Christian. America defines who is an American citizen. Judaism defines who is a Jew, and the acceptance of Jesus as one's messiah puts them outside the walls of Judaism. So, while I respect the rights of those who wish to meld the two traditions into their own faith customs and beliefs, calling themselves Jewish in any way is, to me, inappropriate.

So, I am welcome to attend, but not as a Jew. I received a similar response from another rabbi in town, when I asked for permission to attend services occasionally, "simply as an individual Jew who wants to worship within the Jewish community."

> Dear Russ,
>
> While you are correct as to my opposition to so-called "messianic" Judaism, anyone of any faith is welcome to pray/visit our congregation—so long as they do not proselytize. We have many Christians who visit us.

Both rabbis presented marginalization as the cost of attending services. I can accept such marginalization because I understand its source, and because it may provide a unique opportunity for following Yeshua. This does not mean I can never become more involved in the local Jewish community, but I must start on the margins and prove myself, perhaps mostly by embracing that position. The warning not to proselytize means that we come in suspect and will be under some sort of surveillance by the gatekeepers. But accepting these conditions seems like a fitting posture for a follower of the Messiah who abandoned the center to reveal himself at the margins.

A colleague from South Africa demonstrates this embrace of the margins much more effectively than I have been able to do so far. He writes:

> Recently, I attended a Yizkor service with my brother-in-law on Shavuot. I was the only cohen [priest] present and the gabbai asked me if I would be willing to make an aliyah. I concurred, he took my Hebrew name, and then, in front of the whole shul, the rabbi waved his finger and said no! (somehow, although he was new to the community, my "reputation" had preceded me). And let me tell you, I keep *shtum* [quiet, low-key]. I'm not out on the streets wearing "Jesus made me kosher" t-shirts. But, in such a small community, everyone knows everything about another!
>
> I had to leave the congregation for a few moments so that they could announce "eyn cohen" [no priest is here]. Only then could I reenter and continue with the service. This, ten days after my father's burial. The gabbai came and apologized. Nu, "for I am not ashamed of the . . ." would have been my response, but I held my peace.

This story illustrates a vital reality of life on the margins. Those who are marginalized are tempted to respond by marginalizing others. Thus, the Samaritan woman responds to her marginalization by mocking Yeshua the Jew when he asks her for water. Embracing our place on the margins, rather than merely enduring it, means that we resist this temptation. Though it would doubtless embarrass my South African colleague, he serves as a model for us. South Africa has a significant Jewish community, but it is much smaller and more vulnerable than the Jewish community in the USA. As a more marginalized community, it has perhaps more need to marginalize Messianic Jews. My South African friend accepts his humiliating marginalization with no attempt to marginalize the synagogue. Instead, he leaves the service so that the gatekeepers can announce that there is no cohen present and move on with the service without him. Then, when the presence of a cohen is no longer an issue, he rejoins the congregation for the rest of the service! What irony. He cannot fulfill the role of *cohen* by coming up for an aliyah, but he is still recognized as a *cohen* and must leave the room so that they can declare that there is no cohen present and call someone else to Torah. This local Jewish story provides a symbol for Messianic Jewish marginality and illustrates the guiding ethic on the margins, *hesed*, meaning compassion, faithfulness, and kindness.

Hesed: the ethic of the margins

In one of his encounters with his religious critics, Yeshua tells them, "Those who are well have no need of a physician, but those who are sick. But go and learn what this means: 'I desire mercy and not sacrifice.' For I did not come to call the righteous, but sinners, to repentance" (Matt 9:12–13). Messiah is citing Hosea 6:6, in which "mercy" is *hesed*. He employs the term to characterize his whole ministry of reaching the marginalized—the sick and the sinners—which he sets forth as a model for any who would seek to follow him: "Go and learn what this means: 'I desire *hesed* and not sacrifice.'"

Hesed has been the subject of biblical and theological study for decades. In his watershed 1927 book *Hesed in the Bible*, Nelson Glueck emphasized the connection between *hesed* and *covenant* and portrayed *hesed* as an obligatory part of a covenant relationship. More recently, other scholars have challenged that view. Katherine D. Sakenfeld, for instance, "held in general that *hesed* denotes free acts of rescue or deliverance. . . .'Freedom of decision' is essential. The help is vital, someone is in a position to help, the helper does so in his own freedom and this 'is the central feature in all the texts' (p. 45)." [13] *Hesed* as an act of moral freedom is especially significant for our theme of marginality, as we can see in a number of passages.

---

13. "Hesed" in Theological Wordbook of the Old Testament . . . *citing* Katherine D. Sakenfeld, *The Meaning of Hesed in the Hebrew Bible: A New Inquiry* (Scholars Press, 1978).

At Jacob's well in Samaria, Yeshua initiates an encounter by asking the woman for a drink (John 4:7), just as the servant of Abraham seeks the chosen bride by asking for a drink (Gen 24:14, 17). The servant begins with a prayer:

> ADONAI, God of my master Avraham, please let me succeed today; and show your grace [*hesed*] to my master Avraham (Gen 24:12, CJB). God is the source of *hesed*, but it will be revealed in a human act of kindness freely given. I will say to one of the girls, 'Please lower your jug, so that I can drink.' If she answers, 'Yes, drink; and I will water your camels as well,' then let her be the one you intend for your servant Yitz'chak. This is how I will know that you have shown grace [*hesed*] to my master (Gen 24:14, CJB).

In the event it is an unmarried young woman in a patriarchal society, a woman assigned to the mundane task of drawing water for the household, a woman on the margins who exercises the limited freedom, she has to become the instrument of *hesed*. In doing so she gains tremendous power, becoming the channel of divine choice that will shape the destiny of Abraham's entire line.

When the servant learns that this maiden is of the household of Bethuel, the kinsman of Sarah and Abraham, he says, "Blessed be the Lord God of my master Abraham, who has not forsaken His grace and His truth [*hesed v'emet*] toward my master" (Gen 24:27, NKJV). To underline the divine origin of *hesed*, the text links it with *emet*, here and again in 24:49, as it will be linked later and famously among the thirteen attributes of Exodus 34. *Hesed* is displayed at times by human beings, even those on the margins, but it is ultimately a divine attribute.

The first person called upon in Scripture to practice this attribute is, like Rebecca, a woman in a state of vulnerability. Sarah goes into exile with her husband Abraham, who tells the locals that Sarah is his sister. She is taken into the household of the king. Before the king can touch her, however, God reveals to him in a dream that Sarah is really Abraham's wife. When the king demands an explanation, Abraham claims that Sarah is actually his half-sister, and goes on, "And it came to pass, when God caused me to wander from my father's house, that I said to her, 'This is your kindness [*hesed*] that you should do for me: in every place, wherever we go, say of me, He is my brother'" (Gen 20:13. NKJV). Abraham's request is highly questionable, but he is right in noting that Sarah, in her position of weakness, still has the powerful option of practicing *hesed*.

The prime example of *hesed* as the virtue of the marginal comes in the Book of Ruth. The midrash says, "This scroll tells us nothing either of cleanliness or of uncleanliness, either of prohibition or permission. For what purpose then was it written? To teach how great is the reward of those who do deeds of kindness [*gemilut hasadim*]."[14] *Gemilut hasadim*, of course, employs the plural of *hesed*, so that we might translate it as "bestowals of *hesed*."

Naomi attributes *hesed* to Ruth, along with her sister-in-law Orpah, at the beginning of the book: "And Naomi said to her two daughters in law, Go, return each to her mother's house: The Lord deal kindly [or "in *hesed*"] with you, as you have dealt with the dead and with me" (Ruth 1:8, NKJV). Later, Boaz says: "I have been told of all that you did for your mother-in-law after the death of your husband. . . . May the Lord reward your deeds" (2:11, NJPS). He too comes to describe these deeds as *hesed*, when Ruth presents herself as a marriage partner to him: "Be blessed of the Lord, daughter! Your latest deed of loyalty [*hesed*] is greater than the first, in that you have not turned to younger men, whether poor or rich" (Ruth 3:10, NJPS).

Christians do not ask why the Book of Ruth is in the Scriptures, but rather why Ruth appears in the genealogy of Yeshua (Matt 1:5), which generally follows normal usage and traces Yeshua's descent through the males. Perhaps Ruth is there because she exemplifies *gemilut hasadim*. If so, this links even more strongly the practice of *hesed* with the marginalized. Furthermore, Ruth is not the only woman mentioned in Yeshua's genealogy. There are four others, all marginal figures: Tamar the daughter of Judah, who had to reclaim her neglected rights by posing as a prostitute and enticing her father-in-law to do the right thing (1:3); Rahab (1:5; assuming this is the Rahab of the Book of Joshua [2:1, etc.]); the unnamed wife of Uriah who became the wife of David and bore Solomon (1:6); and Miriam of whom was born Yeshua (1:16). Luke Timothy Johnson summarizes, "[Jesus'] birth to a woman who has conceived by the Holy Spirit (1:20) continues a pattern of God's work among outcast women in Israel."[15]

In his classic work *The New Testament and Rabbinic Judaism*, David Daube demonstrates another connection between Ruth and Miriam. When the angel tells Miriam that she will conceive and bear a son, she asks, "How can this be, since I do not know a man?" The angel replies, "The Holy Spirit will come upon you, and the power of the Highest will overshadow you. . . ." (Luke 1:34–35, NKJV). Daube explains "overshadow" here as an echo of Ruth's request to Boaz: "Take your maidservant under your wing" (Ruth 3:9), showing that the terms for shadow and wing overlap in the targums and early rabbinic literature. The same literature treats the

14. Midrash Rabbah, Vol. 8, 35.

15. Luke Timothy Johnson, *Living Jesus: Learning the Heart of the Gospel* (HarperSanFrancisco: 1999), 147.

Ruth-Boaz relationship as a metaphor for the human-divine relationship, as Ruth the Gentile comes in under the wing of the God of Israel.[16] Daube continues:

> It only remains to add that Mary's words, 'Behold the handmaid of the Lord,' are still from the same source. 'I am Ruth thine handmaid; spread therefore thy wing over thine handmaid,' says Ruth to Boaz. This designation of Mary . . . has its ultimate origins in the Book of Ruth.[17]

The word "handmaid" accentuates Ruth's marginal position, and therefore Miriam's as well. It is *amah* in Hebrew, maidservant, or perhaps even female slave, one needing the protective covering of a powerful male. From this constrained position, Ruth exercises her limited freedom to practice *hesed*, and lays claim to be its prime exemplar in the *Tanakh*.

The practice of *hesed* is not limited to the marginal, of course, but it stands out most dramatically among them. Thus Yeshua calls upon the insiders to learn the practice of *hesed* specifically in the context of his work among the marginalized. Further, Yeshua often practices *hesed* in ways that marginalize him. Thus, he first cites Hosea 6:6, as we have seen, in response to criticism that he eats with tax collectors and sinners. As with the Samaritan woman, Yeshua visits the marginal, and thus marginalizes himself, even drawing the accusation that he is a glutton and a drunkard (Matt 11:19).

We can see *hesed*, then, as the guiding ethic of the marginalized, which we embrace as we embrace our marginalization. The practice of *hesed*, *gemilut hasadim*, reverses the hyper-individualism of our times—the extreme expression of which is marginalization—and hence becomes its cure. Marcus Borg ties Yeshua's instructions on compassion to the Hebrew *rachamim*, rather than *hesed*, but his summary of Yeshua's ethical instruction is apt to our whole discussion:

> Jesus speaks of compassion not only as the primary quality of God, but also as the primary quality of a life lived in accord with God. In remarkably few words, theology and ethics are combined: 'Be compassionate, just as your Father is compassionate' (Luke 6:36). Found in slightly different form in Matthew 5:48, the passage affirms an ethic known as *imitatio dei*, 'imitation of God.'[18]

16. David Daube, *The New Testament and Rabbinic Judaism.* (Peabody, MA: Hendrickson Publishers, 1956), 32–35.

17. Ibid., 36.

18. Marcus J. Borg, *Jesus: Uncovering the Life, Teachings, and Relevance of a Religious Revolutionary* (HarperSanFrancisco, 2006), 175.

A midrash on Deuteronomy 13:5 explores the imitation of God in terms of *gemilut hasadim.*

> What does it mean, 'You shall walk after the Lord your God'? Is it possible for a person to walk and follow in God's presence? Does not the Torah also say 'For the Lord your God is a consuming fire'? (Deut 4:24). But it means to walk after the attributes of the Holy One, Blessed be He. Just as He clothed the naked, so you too clothe the naked, as it says 'And the Lord made the man and his wife leather coverings and clothed them' (Gen 3:21). The Holy One, Blessed be He, visits the ill, as it says, 'And God visited him in Elonei Mamreh (Gen 18:1); so you shall visit the ill. . . .' [Sotah 14a].

By condescending to practice acts of kindness among humankind, God makes the practice of kindness available to all of us, even those on the margins. He also goes out to the margins to practice it, out to the naked, the ill, the bereaved, and the dead. This midrash understands that Torah reveals a God who is not remote and inaccessible, but one who is intimately interacting with human beings. We should not be surprised that this revelation reaches its climax as God comes fully onto the human scene in the person of Yeshua the Messiah. Nor should we be surprised that Messiah is constantly among the sick and needy, embodying acts of kindness in his own ministry and bidding us to follow him in these same acts of kindness, often from his place on the margins. Such practice reverses our marginalization, for we no longer position ourselves among those seeking compassion for themselves (although we can always use it), but as those in a position to provide it.

In recent years the Messianic Jewish community has deepened its practice of *gemilut hasadim* to become involved in humanitarian aid projects within the wider Jewish community, especially in Israel and the former Soviet Union. By practicing *hesed* from the margins we transform our marginality into a position of strength, perhaps more surely than we could through protest or political action. For example, I spent some time on a recent trip to Israel with Avishalom Teklahaimanot, who bears a double marginalization in Israel as a Messianic Jew and as an Ethiopian. Avi is a veteran of several years' service as a social worker and is connected with Ohalei Rachamim congregation. For several years the congregation sought unsuccessfully to work with the local government in providing relief to impoverished Russian and Ethiopian immigrants in the area. During the 2006 war, the municipality asked for help with water supplies, particularly for this needy population. Avi coordinated the congregation's response without making any demands and the municipality soon expanded the cooperation to include help with food and other needs. Thus, this marginalized group, represented by a doubly-marginalized individual, became a provider of resources to those in need.

Return to the Core

A. Reducing incidental marginality

We cannot practice *hesed* in isolation, but only within community, in the context of social relationships where issues of power and status so often prevail. In this setting, as Luke Timothy Johnson reminds us:

> To 'learn Jesus'. . . is not to confuse the present power of the resurrected Jesus with a realized Kingdom in which one deserves a place of authority and privilege. It is instead to learn how to be little and weak, a servant who in the pattern of Jesus gives one's life as a ransom for others.[19]

"Little and weak" is an apt description of today's Messianic Jewish community, even if we would rather be able to describe ourselves as big and strong. Outward circumstances may vary, of course, but marginalization is inherent to life in Yeshua, or to "learning Jesus" as Johnson describes it. We may contrast this inherent marginality with our incidental marginality within the Jewish community, as we have discussed, or in relationship to the Christian community, as we shall consider shortly.

Inherent marginality is most fully expressed in the cross to which Messiah calls his followers, which in the words of John Howard Yoder is "the price of social non-conformity . . . the social reality of representing in an unwilling world the Order to come."[20] Yoder argues throughout his seminal work, *The Politics of Jesus*, that social marginality—not disengagement from society, nor accommodation to it, nor violent resistance against it, but "vulnerable enemy love and renunciation of dominion in the real world"[21]—is essential to the message of Yeshua. Yeshua is announcing a new social order that puts his followers on the margins of the existing order.

Eugene Peterson, writing from a rather different perspective, makes a similar claim:

> North American Christians are conspicuous for going along with whatever the culture decides is charismatic, successful, influential—whatever gets things done, whatever can gather a crowd of followers—hardly notic-

---

19. Johnson, 143.

20. Yoder, *The Politics of Jesus*, 96.

21. Ibid., 132.

ing that these ways and means are at odds with the clearly marked way that Jesus walked and called us to follow. Doesn't anyone notice that the ways and means taken up, often enthusiastically, are blasphemously at odds with the way Jesus leads his followers? Why doesn't anyone notice?[22]

We are not North American Christians, but we too must embrace our inherent marginality in Messiah as an antidote to the cultural blindness of our day. We are to be countercultural, not in the 60s sense of dropping out, but as a prophetic community that lives the message of Torah, particularly as embodied in Yeshua, and particularly as it is at cross-currents with contemporary trends. Something is gravely amiss when the professed followers of Yeshua become the institutional or cultural mainstream.

The Messianic Jewish community's marginality may help us reexamine our relationship to the religious establishment, both Jewish and Christian, and regain the prophetic marginality inherent in following Yeshua. At the same time, we can legitimately seek to reverse our incidental marginality. In a recent paper, Dr. Mitch Glaser defends the return to Jewish identity, in other words the attempt to reverse incidental marginality, in missiological terms.

> We should encourage this return to the core on the part of Messianic Jews. Why? Not simply because it is normal and natural, but also because we hope to reach people in the "core" of the Jewish community—who will only be reached by those Jews returning to the core after being saved on the fringe![23]

Likewise, Glaser speaks of marginalized groups in terms of mission:

> Is it wrong to focus on Telling the Story to these more marginalized groups? No. We should be looking for Jewish people who have not yet found meaning and purpose in life, and might therefore be open to Yeshua. Jesus Himself went to the "lost sheep of the house of Israel" and found greater success among the poor and non-religious than among the "core" members of the Jewish community.[24]

As followers of Yeshua, we embrace our place on the margins, not only because it is inhabited by folks more likely to respond to our message, but because Yeshua is

---

22. Eugene H. Peterson. *The Jesus Way: A Conversation on the Ways that Jesus is the Way* (Grand Rapids, MI: Eerdmans, 2007), 8.

23. Dr. Mitch Glaser, "To Whom Are We Telling the Story?" Paper presented to the Lausanne Consultation on Jewish Evangelism. Hungary. August 2007, 7.

24. Ibid., 5.

uniquely present there. At the same time, we also need to embrace the possibilities of return to the core—of decreasing our incidental marginality. Indeed, maintaining an identity within Israel is essential to the eschatological role of Messianic Jews as the remnant of Israel, which must exist in relationship to the whole. If the remnant becomes completely detached, it ceases to be a remnant. Likewise, the margins only exist in relationship to the core. Even if we remain marginal, we do not disappear. We continue to have a position within the wider sphere of community.

B. Ethical guidelines

Nevertheless, a return to the core raises ethical issues of its own. As we become more involved in Jewish communal activities, attend services and events at local mainstream synagogues more frequently, and learn and pray with other Jews, we need to develop clear standards for how to engage in the right way. If we consider *hesed* as our guiding ethic, how will it help us participate in the wider Jewish community with wisdom and integrity? We can distill at least three guidelines from our discussion so far.

1. Take responsibility for disclosure.

Participation in the 21st century synagogue does not normally imply a particular faith commitment or theological outlook. In most contemporary synagogues it is accepted that the worshipers are there because they are Jews, regardless of their personal beliefs about the nature of God or their understanding of Scripture or tradition. There would seem to be no inherent need for Messianic Jewish worshipers to identify themselves as such in this context, much less in other Jewish communal functions in which they might participate. At the same time, we need to recognize the sensitivities the wider community has toward us and take responsibility for appropriate disclosure. We do not want to be discovered as followers of Yeshua after we have been accepted into community life under the assumption that we are mainstream Jews. We can rightly ask why the community in most aspects is comfortable with Jewish atheists, JuBus, Jewish new agers and all the variations of contemporary Jewish identity, and uniquely stigmatizes us. But *hesed* directs that we accept that reality and respond in peace.

In my case, I felt that I needed to let both rabbis know who I was early on because I am in a visible leadership role within the Messianic Jewish community. Others can go more slowly. But surely when friendships begin to develop, or when we begin to be involved in community life beyond the basic seat-warmer mode, we need to let the appropriate party know who we are. A Messianic Jewish woman might participate in her local Hadassah chapter, for example, but she should let the gatekeepers know who she is before she gets nominated for president.

Yeshua warns us against being ashamed of him and instructs us to stand openly for him. Obviously, wisdom is required, and we have all seen foolishness mislabeled as boldness for Messiah, but we dishonor both the wider Jewish community and our Messiah if we try to hide our loyalty to him for too long.

2. Honor community standards.

This principle obviously relates to the first. Our standards might say that a believer in Yeshua should certainly be more kosher than a professed Jewish atheist, but that is not the community standard at this time. *Hesed* is willing to honor the standards of the community.

In one of my early visits to the synagogue, I was assigned an aliyah. I was eager to participate in the Torah service, but upon reflection realized that I needed to decline. The rabbi was the one who called each person up to the bema, and he knew that I was Messianic. I did not want to put him (or myself) in the awkward position of either calling me up when he did not consider me kosher, or telling me to sit back down in front of the whole congregation. A few months later, after I obtained the rabbi's permission to attend, I was invited to take an aliyah again, and this time I accepted. If the rabbi considered me unkosher, he had been warned and apparently had not seen the need to prevent my coming up.

Jewish identity, of course, is unchangeable. Someone born of a Jewish mother, or converted to Judaism under proper rabbinic authority, remains Jewish whether or not he or she practices any form of Judaism. We would argue *a fortiori* that we remain Jewish because most of us do practice a form of Judaism, and our belief in Yeshua does not change our halachic standing. Still, we need to be sensitive to the *minhag* (local custom). For example, would we want to help constitute a minyan by keeping our identity under wraps in a community that did not consider a believer in Yeshua qualified to be part of a *minyan*? We need to honor community standards, even if we disagree. There will doubtless be times for dissent out of loyalty to Yeshua, but opportunities to express our loyalty will probably come more often through humble service. This brings us to a third point.

3. Serve despite marginalization.

Our South African colleague has provided the illustration for this principle: "I had to leave the congregation for a few moments so that they could announce 'eyn cohen.' Only then could I reenter and continue with the service." Even though he is marginalized unfairly, he refrains from marginalizing the community in return, but instead does what he can to enable it to carry out its service.

We can practice this most simply through financial support of mainstream Jewish efforts (not at the expense, of course, of worthy Messianic Jewish efforts!), being willing to contribute even if we are not fully accepted. As appropriate, this would also apply to volunteer work, and more generally to active loyalty to the Jewish community, which leads to our next section.

These three guidelines admittedly reflect an individual return to the core Jewish community. A greater issue, however, is the communal Messianic Jewish return to the core, even if it is beyond the scope of this paper. For now, we simply recognize that these individual guidelines can be adapted to communal return as well.

On the Christian margins

When I mentioned my occasional visits to a mainstream synagogue to a long-term Christian friend, she expressed some consternation that I was worshiping in a setting that did not acknowledge Jesus as Messiah. Our embrace of marginalization may involve embracing the misunderstanding and distancing of Christian, and even some Messianic Jewish, friends who do not understand our continuing loyalty toward the Jewish people. In the past, allegiance to Yeshua meant acceptance into the mainstream community of Christendom, and attempting to maintain loyalty to the Jewish people at the same time brought marginalization of the severest kind. In our more tolerant age, the marginalization is more subtle, but nonetheless present.

I occasionally meet for prayer with a group of pastors in Albuquerque. A couple of years ago we were discussing the Lausanne Covenant, formulated some 30 years earlier by the International Congress on World Evangelization at Lausanne, Switzerland, as a possible unifying document for our group. When the moderator of the discussion asked if anyone had a problem with any of the language in the Covenant, I had to respond to article 4, "The Nature of Evangelism."

> Jesus still calls all who would follow him to deny themselves, take up their cross, and identify themselves with his new community. The results of evangelism include obedience to Christ, incorporation into his Church and responsible service in the world.[25]

Obviously, this language is not "Messianic," but that was not my objection. Indeed, I was impressed by its full-orbed sense of evangelism as a call to follow Yeshua in self-denial and service to the world. My problem was with two phrases: "identify with his new community," and "incorporation into his Church." I tried to explain to my pastor friends that I understood the biblical significance of these phrases, but incorporation into his Church sounded to my Jewish ears like a call to abandon my Jewish identity and assimilate. Equally troubling, the phrase implies that there is no continuing role or identification as Jews for Jewish Yeshua-believers. Likewise, in article 6, "The Church and Evangelism," the Covenant says, "the Church is at the very center of God's cosmic purpose." My immediate response is to ask where that leaves Israel, a question that risks marginalization in this context, even though these are generous and open-minded men.

The risk of marginalization intensifies if we actually defend traditional Judaism to our Christian friends, and this is surely an aspect of marginalization that we must embrace. Levine speaks of the "popular Christian imagination," which sees Yeshua as the only one in the Jewish world of his day who cares about the poor and marginalized. He is not just against religious leaders who have missed the heart of Torah with their rigorous teaching; rather, in the popular Christian imagination, he is against Torah itself, and ultimately against Judaism.[26] Such a reading may be able to accept that Jews who have not yet found Jesus will cling to their old ways, at least until some final apocalyptic resolution. But Jews who profess loyalty to Yeshua and remain attached to Jewish tradition and community are suspect and risk marginalization.

---

25. "The Lausanne Covenant." Online: http://www.lausanne.org/lausanne-1974/lausanne-covenant .html.

26. Levine, 19.

In response, as always, Yeshua provides our model. He meets the Samaritan woman on the margins, and in some aspects of his conversation with her transcends Jewish-outsider categories, but he also reminds the woman that "Salvation is from the Jews" (John 4:24). Brown interprets this as an expression of Yeshua's loyalty to his people:

> The Jews against whom Jesus elsewhere speaks harshly really refers to that section of the Jewish people that is hostile to Jesus, and especially to their rulers. Here, *speaking to a foreigner*, Jesus gives to the Jews a different significance, and the term refers to the whole Jewish people. This line is a clear indication that the Johannine attitude to the Jews cloaks neither an anti-Semitism of the modern variety nor a view that rejects the spiritual heritage of Judaism.[27]

This, of course, is only one example of Yeshua's loyalty to his people, an example we are to follow in our interactions with the Gentile Christian world, as well as with the secular world. Such a stance, despite the tremendous progress in Jewish-Christian relations in recent years, may threaten our standing or credibility in some Christian circles. It illustrates, however, that *hesed*—loyalty and kindness—characterizes our life on the margins.

Brown's comments hint at a great irony. The Jews, who are often portrayed in the gospels as the gatekeepers and the marginalizers, become the outsiders within Christendom and, as we are often reminded by current events, within modern post-Christendom as well. The Jewish gatekeepers who would marginalize us are acting in part out of their own marginalization, as my friend's experience in South Africa illustrates. Hence, as we embrace our inherent marginality, we must stand in loyalty with the very community that tends to incidentally marginalize us.

Hospitality: communal practice of hesed

A. Synagogue on the margins

Our place on the margins is not just an individual place, but also a communal one, which will be reflected in our congregational polity and culture. This institutional marginality has some advantages. Dr. Ron Wolfson, co-founder of the Synagogue 2000 project, now Synagogue 3000 or S3K, writes about what he terms the "cathedral" synagogue of the past few decades:

---

27. Brown, 172. (Emphasis added.)

> The traditional configuration of synagogues with the Torah reading table in the center of the space was replaced by high pulpits, imposing arks, and regal furniture. Pews were arranged in rows and fixed to the ground, focusing attention squarely on what was happening in the front and reducing the chance for interaction with others. This created distance between the congregants and the clergy, between the people and each other, between the people and their God. In fact, these 'cathedral' synagogues reflected a view of God as transcendent, distant, unapproachable.[28]

The Messianic Jewish community, of course, has not been plagued with imposing arks and regal furniture. Rather, our challenge is to develop meeting places that can be taken seriously by the people we are trying to serve. Still, Wolfson reminds us that limitations can be keys to effectiveness. Indeed, a major premise of S3K has been the need to re-imagine the synagogue, fostering a "paradigm shift away from corporate synagogues as enclaves of ethnicity," and toward synagogue as "a spiritual center for all those who set foot inside it," or a sacred community.[29]

In our contemporary secular age, all congregations—church and synagogue—are marginal. Membership in mainstream groups is declining. It is no longer conventional, that is, expected and beneficial for social standing, but indeed can be a stigma. Borg writes:

> The 'good news' in this decline is that, very soon, the only people left in the mainline congregations will be the ones who are there for intentional and not conventional reasons. This creates the possibility for the church once again to become an alternative community rather than a conventional community. . . .[30]

Borg limits his observation to mainline congregations, but the conventional-intentional contrast applies to more conservative groups as well. Intentional membership means that people join out of conviction, expecting membership to reflect faith and commitment. Messianic Jewish groups have never become established and normative enough to provide conventional reasons for people to join us. Hence, we can embrace our place on the margins of the culture of consumerism and hyper-individualism to become intentional congregations in the best sense.

---

28. Ron Wolfson, *The Spirituality of Welcoming: How to Transform Your Congregation into a Sacred Community* (Woodstock, VT: Jewish Lights, 2005), 18–19.

29. Ibid., 19.

30. Borg, 302–303.

Rabbi Lawrence Hoffman, co-founder with Wolfson of Synagogue 2000, contrasts the dominant market community with sacred community:

> The everyday is what we use as means to ends. The sacred exists as its
> own end. . . . Sacred community . . . is devoted to certain tasks, but these
> can be realized only in a sacred ambience, not in a market community
> where people weigh value by the list of limited liability deliverables that
> they think their dues are buying.[31]

Much good may proceed from a sacred community, but it is not constituted just to get a job done or to provide a collection of programs, projects, and benefits for dues (or tithe) paying consumers. "Congregation" is not a means to an end, but a gathering under Hashem in a shared vision of his holiness and purpose. When a member begins to ask, "what's in it for me?" he or she is already turning back from sacred community into the realm of consumerism.

Within our consumerist culture, sacred community is inherently marginal and this is a marginality that we can embrace. Messianic Jewish marginality is not always a good thing, and does not always arise from sacredness, but neither is it something to be overcome at all costs. Wolfson and Hoffman both spend considerable effort in articulating their vision of sacred community as the goal of synagogue life. Within the Messianic Jewish community, we certainly have not attained such sacred community, but we do not need to be convinced that that is what synagogue life is all about. Put another way, we do not seem to be greatly tempted by the "limited liability" approach that Hoffman decries. Indeed, we probably need to develop more in the direction of offering programs and benefits to members, but we already seem to have accepted the paradigm of congregation as sacred community. In our corporate return to the Jewish core, we need to guard against seeking to become more like the normative synagogues of middle America. Instead, we enter the stream of synagogue renewal from a different point on the shore.

Paradoxically, the congregation, which is inherently marginal within the dominant market community, becomes the place where marginality is overcome. In congregation as sacred community, we both embrace marginality and help others to overcome it—again following the model of Yeshua, who embraced his place on the margins to bring us into the core of God's family. In congregation, we overcome the hyper-individualism of our day, and ironically of much of the religious teaching of our day, which Yoder describes as "radical personalism." In contrast, he writes, "The

---

31. Rabbi Lawrence Hoffman, *Rethinking Synagogues, A New Vocabulary for Congregational Life* (Woodstock, VT: Jewish Lights, 2006), 140.

personhood which [Jesus] proclaims as a healing, forgiving call to all is integrated into the social novelty of the healing community." Yoder continues with words that are particularly relevant to the Messianic Jewish community:

> The idea of Jesus as an individualist or teacher of radical personalism could arise only in the (Protestant, post-Pietist, rationalist) context that it did; that is, in a context which, if not intentionally anti-Semitic, was at least sweepingly a-Semitic, stranger to the Jewish Jesus.[32]

In the congregation, welcome, as in the title of Wolfson's book, *The Spirituality of Welcoming*, provides the transition from margins to core, from individualism to community. The Jewish Jesus teaches us how to welcome not only by welcoming us, but also by needing a welcome himself. He says, "Foxes have holes and birds of the air have nests, but the Son of Man has nowhere to lay his head" (Matt 8:20). This vulnerability positions him to accept the hospitality of a wide array of folk: sinners and tax collectors, unattached women like Marta and Miriam, Pharisees and even leaders of the Pharisees. The opportunity to welcome him draws out the best, and occasionally the worst, of these people. He teaches welcoming, hospitality, by showing up at their door.

At the same time, however, Yeshua does welcome us, for he opens the way into the father's house, which is his house. Thus, he calls us out of the culture of individualism into the "social novelty of the healing community," providing the example for us: "So welcome each other, just as the Messiah has welcomed you into God's glory" (Rom 15:7, CJB). Welcoming, like *hesed*, is inherent to life on the margins. Indeed, welcoming within the congregation is a bestowal of *hesed*[1] on the communal level.

B. *The welcoming synagogue*

Radical hospitality characterizes Yeshua's entire way of life. In the Messianic Jewish community, we face the dilemma of practicing such hospitality at the same time as maintaining a legitimate Jewish distinctive. When Wolfson speaks of the synagogue as "a spiritual center for all those who set foot inside it," he can hardly imagine the wide range of those who might set foot inside a Messianic synagogue. Because Yeshua is the focal point of our communal life, our congregations attract many more Gentiles than do mainstream synagogues, sometimes even Gentiles hardly familiar with Jewishness at all. How do we respond to such individuals without violating radical hospitality on the one hand or Jewish values and priorities on the other?

---

32. Yoder, 108–109.

Resolving this dilemma is beyond the scope of this paper and may indeed be the task of a generation to come. For now, I offer three suggestions. First, we must be careful not to invalidate the attraction that these Gentiles feel toward the Messianic synagogue. They may misconstrue it as a restoration of the true, first-century congregation, a place where they can reconnect with the "Jewish roots" from which the church became tragically detached. But often at the heart of their attraction is a yearning for God and Scripture that we should honor, even if we need to redirect it. Second, we can build alliances with a few churches that have a healthy attitude toward Jewish roots and Israel and could provide a good home for Gentile believers disenchanted with other sorts of churches. We can welcome them as visitors to our congregations, and provide helpful direction in finding a permanent home. Third, we can affirm *chavurot*, which inherently have a more defined welcome than a larger, public gathering, that are committed to an intentional Jewish focus. Such *chavurot* might even be connected to a larger Messianic congregation that practices a broader and less qualified welcome, and therefore has a more diverse membership.

Organizing our congregations so that hospitality does not threaten distinct Jewish calling should help us to practice a more radical hospitality. Wolfson asks, "How can a synagogue love guests? The single most important way is for the congregation members themselves to express their personal welcome when they see a stranger."[33] This is most likely to occur in a congregation that has learned hospitality as a core value, and that has developed ways not to become overwhelmed by the strangers.

Beyond these concerns, hospitality provides an alternative to the dominant values of individualism and consumerism. Just as hospitality is "not about me," but about the stranger who shows up at the door, so it reminds us that the congregational gathering is not about me. Worship is not another commodity to be experienced and enjoyed, but the activity above all others that is about God. Our congregational services and structures need to reflect this renunciation of consumerism and individualism. They should not be designed to serve the religious needs of members, as much as to inspire members in worship, outreach, and redemptive social engagement.

Radical hospitality requires not only welcoming the marginalized through our doors, but extending ourselves to the margins where they live. Welcoming the visitor, then, is not about congregational growth, even if this is a worthy goal, but, as David Rudolph states, "is an ethic that is central to the character, shape, and calling

---

33. Wolfson, 52.

of our community."[34] Indeed, we need to guard against developing the congregation as a place of welcome in ways that would exempt us from practicing hospitality in our own homes and personal lives. Instead, the individual practice of hospitality is essential to overcoming deeply rooted sins of our culture such as materialism, consumerism, and exaltation of self. Likewise, we need to guard against thinking that outward practices of welcome can alone address the issue. Welcome must be a part of the radical otherness of Yeshua's community, a contrast with the dominant response to the outsider based on status, power, and image.

The paragon of hospitality in the Torah, of course, is Abraham, whom Rudolph labels "hospitality man."[35] In the paradigmatic story of Abraham's hospitality, he sees three men standing before him as he sits in his tent door in the heat of the day. One of the three turns out to be the angel of the Lord, indeed the Lord, Hashem, himself, for this story is announced with the words "Vayera—And the Lord appeared to him . . . ." (Gen 18:1). When Hashem appears, he is in need of hospitality. He teaches us to welcome by leaving his central place to appear on the margins, just as the Son of Man appears to tax collectors, Pharisees and marginal women in need of hospitality.

The Son of Man is also prefigured in this story by Abraham. Like Messiah, Abraham is both central to the whole story and positioned on its margins. He lives in the land of promise, but he is a sojourner there, dwelling in tents that have no permanent foundation. By renouncing the present-day center, he declares his hope in the future fulfillment of all God's promises. Marginality is not a tactical maneuver to enhance our effectiveness in today's world, but a position of protest and hope. It is inherent to walking with Messiah away from the values and means that dominate the age in which we live for the sake of something better.

Abraham reminds us that welcome may entail an encounter with Yeshua, who often shows up among those who appear at our doors. From the margins, Abraham welcomes the divine presence and from the same margins, Hashem reveals himself and his purposes to his faithful servant. May such encounters be ours as well!

RUSSELL RESNIK serves as Executive Director of the Union of Messianic Jewish Congregations, has an international teaching and speaking ministry, and is the author of *Divine Reversal, Gateways to Torah* and *Creation to Completion.*

---

34. David Rudolph, "Abraham, Hospitality Man" in *Kesher: A Journal of Messianic Judaism* 21 (Summer/Fall 2006): 2.

35. Ibid., 3.

Moses on the Mountain and the Motifs of Heavenly Ascent*

Andrew Sparks

Moses is a biblical figure of primary significance in the Torah. One expression of Moses' importance is his intimacy with God. On numerous occasions, Moses finds himself in God's immediate presence. In each instance of theophany, Moses ascends a mountain to encounter God.

These accounts of theophany share features common to the literary phenomenon of heavenly ascents. Specifically, Moses' heavenly ascents contain a complex of motifs shared by ascent accounts in biblical, Second Temple, and rabbinic literature. In the history of interpretation, these motifs associated with Moses' ascents are reworked and adapted to fit various social contexts.

One such exegetical motif, which has not received a great deal of attention yet appears in a broad range of witnesses, is the law mediated by angels. The LXX and Targums, the Pseudepigrapha and Apocrypha, Philo, Josephus, the NT,[1] and rabbinic literature all seem to bear witness to the motif. In fact, Strack and Billerbeck list many occurrences of the motif (*Verordnet durch Engel*).[2] Although the presence of the motif throughout Second Temple literature seems undeniable, some scholars fail to recognize even the presence of this motif in Jewish literature. L. Gaston asserts, "That the Law was given to Israel by angels must be called exclusively a Pauline concept, if indeed that is what Paul says."[3] The following development of the motif from its biblical nexus, *viz.*, Deut 33:2 and Ps 68:17, to later forms in Second Temple and

* Paper originally presented at the Society of Biblical Literature Regional Conference (Eastern Great Lakes) March 23, 2006.

1. See Acts 7:38, 53; Gal 3:19; and Heb 2:2.

2. "Die Engel setzten den Israeliten das Gesetz u. die Tragweite seiner einzelnen Bestimmungen auseinander. Josephus, Antiq 15,5,3 läßt den Herodes sagen: Was Hellenen u. Barbaren übereinstimmend für das Frevelhafteste halten, das haben sie (die Araber) unsren Gesandten angetan, indem sie sie hinmordeten, da doch die Hellenen die Herolde für heilig u. durch Engel von Gott δι- ἀγγέλων παρὰ τοῦ θεοῦ gelernt haben" (Hermann L. Strack and Paul Billerbeck, *Kommentar Zum Neuen Testament und Midrash*, vol. 3 (München: C.H. Beck, 1926), 556).

3. L. Gaston, "Angels and Gentiles in Early Judaism and in Paul," *Studies in Religion* 11, no.1 (1982): 67. See also L. Ginzberg, *An Unknown Jewish Sect* (New York: Jewish Theological Seminary of America, 1976), 172–74.

rabbinic literature offers an alternative accounting of the evidence. As a result, the most comprehensive treatment of the trajectory of the motif to date is provided.

Motif-analysis

A systematic approach to the treatment of motifs is necessary to proceed. Motif-analysis accounts for the developments and variances in motifs.[4] The analytical method seeks to uncover the interpretive history of a motif by taking into consideration the social context and diverse ideologies reflected by each occurrence. Through careful examination of textual modification, motif-analysis meets the need for evaluation of a tradent's influence upon a motif. Motif-analysis incorporates three types of semantic accent: acceptance, emphasis and resistance. Ancient writers accepted, emphasized or resisted motifs from pre-existing texts or traditions based on their own ideology and the conceptuality of their communities.

Motif-analysis may effectively be applied to heavenly ascents literature, and in particular, to the motif of the law mediated by angels. These motifs are analyzed along the lines of semantic accent and a determination is made whether a pre-existing motif has been accepted, emphasized, or resisted in a text. Motif-analysis also incorporates the following tasks:

1. Establish the social and textual context of the motif in biblical and extra-biblical literature.

2. Analyze the use of the motif in biblical and extra-biblical literature.

3. Determine the purpose and function of the motif in biblical and extra-biblical literature.

Moses' Mountain Ascents

The early history of the modern study of ascents, stemming from the *Religiongeschichteschule*, recognized heavenly ascents in the context of anthropology. As ascent texts were associated with many cultures and approached from various disciplines, the texts reflected shared structural and stylistic features. Although

---

4. An adaptation of motif-analysis has been applied by the author to the field of text criticism in "The Servant Songs of Isaiah: Contrasting Ideologies and Conflicting Texts," unpublished thesis (New Haven, CT: Yale University, 1999). This text-critical approach ascertains the theological perspective of a textual tradent by examining the modification of texts. By narrowing the traditional distinction between a copyist/translator and exegete, the method treats the interpretive stance of a tradent, not as an addendum to text criticism, but as pertinent data for textual analysis.

these common features do not merit a generic claim, the literary patterns and shared motifs of ascent texts allow for comparison and contrast. Part of the contribution of motif-analysis is to show both commonalities and distinctions between the texts of Moses' mountain ascents and heavenly ascent literature.

Two major types of ascents are those which are followed by a return to earth and ascents which occur at death. Due to Moses' prominence in the Torah, he experiences both types of ascent. Ex 19–20 and Deut 4–5 interact with the first type[5] and Deut 34 is the basis of the tradition of Moses' ascent at death.

The parallel accounts in Exodus and Deuteronomy refer to the theophany at Mt. Sinai. This mountain ascent is distinct from much of heavenly ascent literature in that there is a meeting half-way. The ascent does not proceed to heaven, for God comes down to earth. In this sense, there is a meeting of heaven and earth on a cosmic mountain as God offers revelation to Israel. In fact, the cosmic mountain in Moses' ascent texts may be the paramount motif.

Across various cultures and times, people have perceived physical structures standing between heaven and earth. These structures have been utilized to symbolize ascents and take the form of climbing ropes, trees, and ladders.[6] Yet, the most prevalent physical structure in the biblical tradition is the mountain. From Mt. Moriah to Mt. Sinai, and from Mt. Nebo to Mt. Zion, God spoke and acted.

Mt. Sinai, also called Mt. Horeb, is a focal point of Moses' mountain ascents and refers to the mountain district which was reached by Israel in the third month after the Exodus. Here, Israel remained encamped for a year. The last twenty-two chapters of Exodus, together with the whole of Leviticus and Numbers 1–11, contain a record of all which occurred at Mt. Sinai.

Mt. Nebo is the locus of the second type of ascent associated with Moses.[7] Deuteronomy assigns great importance to Moses' final ascent at death on Mt. Nebo. The event prepares Israel for new leadership and a new homeland.[8] This original significance of the event does not fade with time. Although Deuteronomy only records the burial of Moses by God, motifs of heavenly ascent found a home in the account

---

5. Cf. Neh 9:13–14.

6. E.g., Gen 28:12 for the account of Jacob who saw angels 'ascending and descending' upon a cosmic ladder.

7. Mt. Nebo has been identified with Jebel Nebah, on the eastern shore of the Dead Sea, near its northern end, in the land of Moab.

8. Dennis T. Olsen highlights the pivotal significance of Moses' death in *Deuteronomy and the Death of Moses: A Theological Reading* (Minneapolis: Fortress Press, 1994).

of Moses' death.[9] These motifs attached themselves to the extra-biblical accounts and engendered the transformation of a burial tradition into a heavenly ascent.[10]

The use of the mountain motif in both types of Moses' ascents reflects a transcultural perception of mountains as a place of theophany. R.J. Clifford in his study on cosmic mountains explains:

> In the ancient civilizations from Egypt to India and beyond the mountain can be a center of fertility, the primeval hillock of creation, the meeting place of the gods, the dwelling place of the high god, the meeting place of heaven and earth, the monument effectively upholding the order of creation, the place where god meets man, a place of theophany.[11]

Clifford then expands on the ancient understanding of theophany:

> In the religions of the Ancient Near East, to characterize rather broadly, divine presence was sought not so much in a mystical inward searching of the soul but in symbolism where a relationship was established between the natural and supernatural worlds. By means of their form or shape, or some other indefinable quality, earthly objects symbolized or made present the gods or their abodes.[12]

For Israel, the cosmic mountain becomes the quintessential dwelling place of the divine and the locus of heavenly ascents. Clifford summarizes the connection between Israel's adoption of the cosmic mountain motif and similar conceptions of the surrounding nations.

> The Canaanite storm-god, Baal-Hadad, lives on Mount Zaphon. Zaphon, like Zion, is the scene of battle, is ultimately impregnable, is the place where the deity has his temple/palace and exercises kingship, and so on. Even Mount Sinai, the mountain of law-giving, stands in the Canaanite tradition of the cosmic mountain.[13]

9. E.g., Jude 9 records a dispute that arose over the body of Moses.

10. This textual phenomenon reflects James Kugel's fifth hermeneutical principle: "One exegetical motif can influence the creation or development of another" (James L. Kugel, *In Potiphar's House: The Interpretive Life of Biblical Texts* [San Francisco: HarperSanFrancisco, 1990], 247–70).

11. Richard J. Clifford, *The Cosmic Mountain in Canaan and the Old Testament* (Cambridge, Mass.: Harvard University Press, 1972), 5.

12. Ibid., 6.

13. Ibid., 4.

Another prominent motif in heavenly ascent literature relates to angelic mediators. Angelic beings serve as mediators by either helping or hindering a heavenly ascent, or by mediating a divine message. In the case of Moses' mountain ascents, a recurring motif is the law mediated by angels. In order to shed light on this motif, the primary settings for the development of the tradition need to be explored. Then, once the broader contextual horizons of Deuteronomy and the Second Temple period are established, the motif can be examined in its distinct forms in extra-biblical literature.

The Biblical Context of Moses' Mountain Ascents

One step in recognizing the place of Moses' ascents and its corresponding motifs is an orientation to the canonical context. One possible canonical center of the Hebrew Bible is theophany. It has been argued that the narrative flow of much of the Hebrew Bible turns on theophany, mainly represented by mountain ascents. D.L. Christensen offers this perspective:

> In each of its two halves the primary epic story takes on a threefold structure within the canonical process in ancient Israel by the insertion of theophanic visitations, first to Moses and subsequently to Elijah-on the same mountain (Exod 33–34; 1 Kgs 19). The Exodus involves a journey from Yam Suf (Sea Of Reeds) to the Jordan River in three stages. The great theophany at Sinai . . . framed, on the one hand, by the wilderness journey from Egypt to Sinai and, on the other, by the wilderness journey from Sinai to Mount Nebo and the transfer of leadership from Moses to Joshua . . . . A parallel structure can be seen within the so-called Deuteronomic History Joshua through 2 Kings. Here the journey is from 1) the desert to the promised land symbolized as a mountain, to 2) central theophanies on Mount Carmel (1 Kgs 18) and Mount Horeb (1 Kgs 19) . . . and 3) the journey to Mount Zion as the city of God, particularly as seen in the climactic reforms of Hezekiah (2 Kgs 18-20) and Josiah (2 Kgs 22-23).[14]

Theophany and heavenly ascent also underlie Israel's temple worship and subsequent synagogue worship service. Worship in ancient Israel imitates and re-enacts heavenly ascent.[15] The Psalms of Ascent beckon, "Who may ascend the heavenly hill?" As the people ascend Mt. Zion, the heavenly mount, they encounter God.

---

14. Duane L. Christensen, *Deuteronomy 1–11*, Word Biblical Commentary (Dallas, Texas: Word Books, 1991), lii.

15. Liturgical recital is prescribed: "Only give heed to yourself and keep your soul diligently, so that

In one account, Israel ascends to the Temple mount and Solomon prays to dedicate the First Temple. As a result, the Divine presence descends and fills the Temple. Sinai and Zion are connected and display theophany, an approximation of heavenly ascent.[16] G. von Rad describes the Israelite worship experience:

> Consider Ps. 50 . . . We are forced to postulate here a cultic ritual of a similar if not identical kind to that presupposed by the Sinai narrative. The assembly stands in anticipation of a theophany, the climax of which is an allocation by God himself. The cultic community had been called together by God and sacrifices have been offered.[17]

In each case of theophany, God comes in the midst of the angelic assembly.[18] Deut 33:1–3 briefly describes the Mt. Sinai theophany. The heavenly divine counsel and the earthly assembly are linked as the Lord of the 'assembly of Jacob' is accompanied by the angels of heaven. Israel is gathered before the mountain in holy array and all the holy ones are present.

Moses' mountain ascents are also foundational to Deuteronomy's formation. According to the narrative of Deuteronomy, the book is a record of pre-existing laws delivered by God at Mt. Sinai and recounted by Moses forty years later. Because Israel was too frightened by the theophany to hear God present the remaining stipulations, God communicated them only to Moses.[19] These stipulations were then transmitted to the people shortly before Moses' death. Moses then reconfirmed the Sinai covenant with a second covenant covering these additional stipulations.[20]

---

you do not forget the things which your eyes have seen and they do not depart from your heart all the days of your life; but make them known to your sons and your grandsons. Remember the day you stood before the Lord your God at Horeb, when the Lord said to me, 'Assemble the people to Me, that I may let them hear My words so they may learn to fear Me all the days they live on the earth, and that they may teach their children'" (Deut 4:9–10).

16. Jon D. Levenson, *Sinai and Zion: An Entry Into the Jewish Bible* (San Francisco: Harper, 1985).

17. Gerhard von Rad, *The Problem of the Hexateuch and Other Essays* (Edinburgh: Oliver & Boyd, 1966), 25. Von Rad further captures the sense of a Sinai tradition driven by and culminating in theophany: "The constitutive element of the Sinai tradition is the coming of God, not the wanderings of the people" (p. 20).

18. Images of angelic presence figure prominently in Israel's worship setting. For example, cherubim are placed on top of the ark and are embroidered on the Tabernacle's curtains.

19. Deut 5:19–6:3.

20. The core of Deuteronomic law recorded in chapters 12–26 is introduced by narrative (chapters 1–4) and admonitions (chapters 5–11) and then sanctioned by promises and warnings (chapters 27–28).

Moses' mountain ascent is also set in the context of the reception of the Decalogue. Both Deuteronomy 4–5 and Exodus 19–20 demonstrate an analogous shaping of the material as each law code is introduced by the Decalogue. Even so, two ways of distinguishing God's presence exist in Exodus and Deuteronomy. The Deuteronomic representation of Moses' mountain ascent is tailored to present a distinct, yet complementary type of monotheism.

Deuteronomy 4–5 sets a trajectory by introducing a recurring central theme concerning idolatry. It begins in chapter 4, a speech replete with idol polemic.[21] According to Deuteronomy, no other god exists except Adonai.[22] Exclusive monotheism is demanded. This monotheizing approach and iconoclastic spirit of Deuteronomy offers a prescribed way for reading Moses' mountain ascent. In fact, Deuteronomy's version of Moses' mountain ascent may be the lens through which the Exodus version is to be read.

Since Deuteronomy advances pre-existing Tetrateuchal traditions, then the final redactor of the Pentateuch may intend for Deuteronomy to function as the reading strategy of the whole.[23] Thus, the Deuteronomist provides contrast. While Exodus records that Moses saw God,[24] in Deuteronomy, Moses only heard God's voice and did not see God's form. This unseen and invisible depiction of deity logically prohibits any representation of the divine being.[25] Furthermore, in Deuteronomy, God is ideally localized at the chosen worship center.[26] Yet, in Exodus, God is mobile and can make the divine name dwell in many places.

In the ancient Near East, local deities spread to other regions and syncretism was a natural phenomenon. There were many *elim* of various places, including *El* of Ugarit and Haran. Into this religious context, an ascent which represented the deity as localized in one place, yet without form would distinguish the God of Israel from foreign competitors. Deuteronomy is uncompromising.[27]

---

21. Deuteronomy 4:3–4 references a history lesson on idolatry harkening back to Num 25:1–13: "Your eyes have seen what the Lord has done in the case of Baal-peor . . . ."

22. Deut 4:35.

23. Evidence of dependence includes the reverse chronology of the wilderness account in Deuteronomy 1–5, culminating in Mount Sinai theophany.

24. See Ex 20:18. For a detailed discussion of other differences in the accounts of Exodus and Deuteronomy, see Brevard S. Childs, *The Book of Exodus* (The Westminster Press, Louisville, 1976), 361.

25. Deut 4:12.

26. Deut 12:5–7.

27. "So watch yourselves, that you do not forget the covenant of the Lord your God which He made

The Extra-Biblical Context of Moses' Mountain Ascents

Moses' mountain ascents and the motif of the law mediated by angels occur in the works of Josephus, Philo, the New Testament, and rabbinic literature. These representative texts illuminate the use of Moses' ascents during the post-biblical periods and incorporate biblical citations or allusions into a variety of motifs. The Pseudepigrapha and Apocrypha, one source of these motifs, functions as a theological and hermeneutical backdrop to the texts that reference Moses' ascents.[28]

One social force which influences the portrayal of Moses' ascents is the interplay of community and culture. In Second Temple Judaism, a Hellenistic crisis arose. Jewish communities struggled to maintain their unique identities while adapting to Greek culture. Hellenization, though, also allowed for a Judaizing process. Jewish culture made its mark on the Greeks as Greek thought and culture became semitized in Jewish hands. One center of Hellenistic influence was Alexandria, the likely birthplace of the Septuagint and a city with a large Jewish community. It became a place of the meshing of two cultures. The writings of Josephus and Philo reflect the intermixing of these two cultures on a conceptual and linguistic level.

Philo's view of divine law is a good place to explore conceptual ties to the motif of the law mediated by angels. In this early first-century context, Philo offers a polemic for Jewish law.[29] E. Goodenough comments:

---

with you, and make for yourselves a graven image in the form of anything against which the Lord your God has commanded you. For the Lord your God is a consuming fire, a jealous God. When you become the father of children and children's children and have remained long in the land, and act corruptly, and make an idol in the form of anything, and do that which is evil in the sight of the Lord your God so as to provoke Him to anger, I call heaven and earth to witness against you today, that you will surely perish quickly from the land where you are going over the Jordan to possess it. You shall not live long on it, but will be utterly destroyed. The Lord will scatter you among the peoples, and you will be left few in number among the nations where the Lord drives you. There you will serve gods, the work of man's hands, wood and stone, which neither see nor hear nor eat nor smell" (Deut 4:23–26).

28. Works that treat the interpretive realm of the Pseudepigrapha and Apocrypha include: Craig Evans and William F. Stinespring, eds., *Early Jewish and Christian Exegesis: Studies in Memory of William Hugh Brownlee* (Atlanta: Scholars Press, 1987); James Charlesworth and W.P. Weaver, eds., *The Old and New Testaments: Their Relationship and the "Intertestamental" Literature* (Valley Forge, PA: Trinity Press International, 1993); James Charlesworth, ed., *The Old Testament Pseudepigrapha*, vols. 1 & 2 (Garden City, NY: Doubleday, 1983); D.A. Carson and H.G.M. Williamson, eds., *It Is Written: Scripture Citing Scripture: Essays in Honour of Barnabas Lindars* (Cambridge: Cambridge University Press, 1988); and Devorah Dimant, "Use and Interpretation of Mikra in the Apocrypha and Pseudepigrapha," in *Mikra: Text, Translation, Reading and Interpretation of the Hebrew Bible in Ancient Judaism and Early Christianity*, ed. M.J. Mulder and H. Sysling (Philadelphia: Fortress Press, 1988), 379–419.

29. Cf. Josephus' defense of Judaism with reference to law in *Against Apion* 2:145–296.

> When one turns to Philo's notion of Jewish Law it is clear that Jewish apol-
> ogetic fervor has been the inspiration of this intensified stress upon Law
> in general. By magnifying Law, and by orienting Jewish Law with Natural
> Law as the Law of God, the Jew could present his religion as the solution of
> the Greek problem, or of the mystic search of the Hellenistic Age.[30]

Philo makes Judaism a viable solution for the Greeks by aligning biblical law with natural law and by submitting Judaism to the dictates of human reason. Philo understood that Judaism has, at its deepest meaning, a correspondence with Greek thought.

In Josphus' presentation of Judaism to the Romans, Judaism is also adapted to Greek ideals. The great biblical figures including Moses are molded to fit the Greek epic tradition of great heroes like Hercules. For Josephus, Moses is another 'hero' recast in the mold of Hercules.[31] Josephus and Philo paraphrase and revise and, as a result, allow for a blending of Hellenism and Judaism.

The early social context of Rabbinic Judaism also functions as a backdrop to later ascent texts. By the second century CE, the pluralism of Judaism known in previous centuries gave way to a pharisaic lay movement. The presenting problem was the need for stability after the destruction of the Temple. A stabilization process began as speculation about God's near deliverance subsided. The Judaisms of the first century became Rabbinic Judaism, a formative Judaism. A non-apocalyptic approach to the community's future emerged as Jewish leadership perpetuated survival by maintaining status quo. Apocalyptic motifs from pseudographical and apocryphal writings were resisted and eschatological speculation diminished in Rabbinic Judaism.

Examples of resistance to apocalyptic texts and motifs of heavenly ascent abound in Rabbinic tradition. In the Palestinian Talmud, the study of Ezekiel is restricted as apocalypic texts began to be regarded as dangerous texts. As early as 200 CE, when the Mishna was codified, R. Yehuda, a rationalist, resisted heavenly ascents and shifted the Jewish perspective of these accounts.[32] Some of the pre-

---

30. Edwin R. Goodenough, *By Light, Light* (New Haven: Yale University Press, 1935), 72. Philo's approach to biblical texts is delineated by Goodenough: "To Philo the first chapters of Genesis have for their purpose the implication that the cosmos sing in harmony with the Law and the Law with the cosmos, and that the law-abiding man is forthwith a citizen of the cosmos, for he is one who regulates his actions in accordance with the will of nature . . ." (p. 49).

31. *Jewish War* 3:399–404.

32. As a corollary, messianism is resisted in the Mishna. For further discussion, see Craig A. Evans, "Mishna and Messiah 'in Context': Some Comments on Jacob Neusner's Proposals," JBL 112 (1993): 267ff.

existing heavenly ascent accounts survived in the Tosefta, yet were critiqued in later Talmudic development.[33]

As could be anticipated, the anti-apocalyptic tendency led to resistance of the motif of the law mediated by angels. In contrast, Nazarene messianism during the pre-Rabbinic period perpetuated and developed the apocalyptic tradition. The New Testament accepts the motif of the law mediated by angels with allusions in Acts 7:38, 53, Gal 3:19 and Heb 2:2.

A comparison of the hermeneutics of Josephus, Philo, and the rabbis further explains the impact of social forces on biblical traditions and the motifs of heavenly ascent. For Philo, the allegorical method predominated and allowed him to change the meaning of the text without necessarily altering the form of biblical texts. Josephus' approach was to paraphrase the biblical text. This strategy lent itself to a reworking of the text in accordance with an apologetic motive.[34] Josephus sought to cultivate empathy for Judaism among the Gentiles through a refined Greek revision of the Septuagint. For the early rabbis as well, interpretive procedure and the revision of texts provided the means to stabilize and reformulate Judaism in the wake of the destruction of the Temple in the first century, and expulsion in the second century.

In summary, Philo and Josephus remodeled Judaism largely in response to *external* cultural forces and ideology, while Rabbinic Judaism reacted to *internal* social dilemmas by developing indigenous traditions. The former sought to change from the outside-in and the later changed from the inside-out. Regardless, change resulted in new meaning and perspectives on the biblical text including Moses' ascents.

The Motif of the Law Mediated by Angels

The motif of the law mediated by angels occurs in Josephus' portrayal of Moses' ascent. In Antiquities 15:136, a passage which references Moses' ascent at Mt. Sinai, angelic mediation is stipulated.

ἃ γὰρ ὁμολογεῖται παρανομώτατα τοῖς τε Ἕλλησιν καὶ τοῖς βαρβάροις, ταῦτα ἔπραξαν εἰς τοὺς ἡμετέρους πρέσβεις, ἀποσφάξαντες αὐτούς, τῶν με Ἑλλήνων ἱεροὺς καὶ ἀσύλους

---

33. See y. *Chag.* 2:1, the account of the four who entered the garden and b. *Chag.* 15a.

34. Harold Attridge, *The Interpretation of Biblical History in the Antiquities Judaicae of Flavius Josephus* (Missoula: Scholars Press, 1976), 69–70. Attridge captures the purposefulness and design of Josephus' use of sources. He states, "The *Antiquities* draws on a variety of sources, biblical and non-biblical, but it does not simply copy them. Rather, it elaborates them according to fairly clear patterns."

εἶναι τοὺς κήρυκας φαμένων, ἡμῶν δε τὰ κάλλιστα τῶν δογμάτων
καὶ τὰ ὁσιώτατα τῶν ἐν τοῖς νόμοις δι' ἀγγέλων παρὰ τοῦ θεοῦ
μαθόντων· τοῦτο γὰρ τὸ ὄνομα καὶ ἀνθρώποις θεὸν εἰς ἐμφάνειαν
ἄγειν καὶ πολεμίους πολεμίοις διαλλάττειν δύναται.[35]

For these men [Arabs] have done what both the Greeks and Barbarians
own to be an instance of the grossest wickedness, with regard to our ambassadors, whom they have beheaded, while the Greeks declare that such
ambassadors are sacred and inviolable. And for ourselves, we have learned
the most excellent of our doctrines, and the most holy part of our law from
the angels sent by God. For this name [ambassadors] brings God to men,
and is sufficient to reconcile enemies one to another.[36]

The motif of the law mediated by angels in *Ant* 15:136 allows Josephus, by
means of Herod's speech, to support the claim that 'ambassadors are sacred and
inviolable.' The motive for the inclusion of the motif fits into the larger purpose
for Herod's speech. Herod's speech (*Ant* 15:127–46) is designed to encourage his
troops to defeat the Arabs in battle, which they eventually do on two occasions (*Ant*
15:147–60). The troops are mustered to destroy enemies who are 'unjust toward
friendship, truce-violators in battle, and sacrilegious toward envoys' (*Ant* 15:146).
Jews, like the Greeeks, recognize this policy toward ambassadors since they received
their law from ἀγγέλων.

The identity of ἀγγέλων has been disputed, even though a literal reading
makes sense in the context of *Ant* 15:147–60.[37] W.D. Davies holds that ἀγγέλων
may refer to prophets rather than angelic beings.[38] Many interpreters have followed
in Davies' footsteps, including L. Silberman:

It is important to note Davies's tentative conclusion concerning the issue:
Because of the well attested tradition that the Law was given by angels it

35. Henry St. J. Thackeray et al., eds., *Josephus* (London: Heinemann, 1926–1965 [*Ant* 15:136 can
be found in Vol. VI, pp. 320–322, translated by Ralph Marcus and edited by Allen Wikgren]).

36. Author's translation.

37. Although Allen Wikgren, in a editorial note in the Loeb Classical Library, takes ἀγγέλων to
mean prophets by comparing *Ap.* i:37, most translate the Greek as angels (p. 322). In Wikgren's citation
of *Against Apion*, Josephus uses the Greek for prophets and identifies them as recipients of inspiration
and not mediators of law. Marcus' translation of 'messengers' for ἀγγέλων not only veers from a literal
rendering, but obscures the presence of the motif of the law mediated by angels within the text.

38. W.D. Davies, "A Note on Josephus, Antiquities 15:136," *HTR* 97 (1954): 135–40.

is natural to find the idea here in Josephus, but the following factors may justify a reference instead to the prophets as ambassadors of God.[39]

One Midrashic tradition that equates the prophets with the designation, 'angels,' is recorded in Midrash Wayyiqra Rabbah:

> The prophets are called angels as it is written: 'and he sent an angel and he brought us forth from Egypt' (Num 2.16). Now was it an angel? From this it is evident that prophets were called angels.[40]

A. Bandstra makes a cogent rebuttal to Davies' position. He responds first to Silberman's argument by saying, "by the time of Josephus, the word *angelos* was sometimes used to refer to a prophet or a priest. That, however, does not decide the case in Josephus; it only makes that interpretation possible."[41] Bandstra's offers additional counter-argument to Davies' position:

> Furthermore, Davies's argument has only the weight of an *argumentum e silencio*. The counterpart to this argument from silence is another argument from silence—namely, that Josephus nowhere uses the term *angeloi* to refer to the canonical prophets.[42]

The motif of the law mediated by angels may be traced either directly or indirectly to biblical sources. The first potential occurrences of the motif are found in the texts and versions of Deut 33:2 and Ps 68:17.

MT Deut 33:2

וַיֹּאמַר יְהוָה מִסִּינַי בָּא וְזָרַח מִשֵּׂעִיר לָמוֹ הוֹפִיעַ מֵהַר פָּארָן וְאָתָה מֵרִבְבֹת
קֹדֶשׁ מִימִינוֹ אֵשׁדָּת לָמוֹ

LXX Deut 33:2

καὶ εἶπεν Κύριος ἐκ Σινὰ ἥκει, καὶ ἐπέφανεν ἐκ Σηιῆμιν καὶ κατέσπευσεν ἐξ
ὄρους Φαρὰν σύν μυριάσιν Καδῆς, ἐκ δεξιῶν αὐτοῦ ἄγγελοι μετ' αὐτοῦ.

---

39. L. Silberman, "Prophets/Angels: LXX Qumran Psalm 151 and the Epistle to the Hebrews," in *Standing Before God: Studies on Prayer in Scriptures and in Tradition with Essays*, ed. Asher Finkel and Lawrence Frizzell (New York: Ktav Publishing House, Inc., 1981), 100, n.16.

40. Mordecai Margulies, *Midrash Wayyiqra Rabbah: A Critical Edition based on manuscripts and Genizah fragments with variants and notes* (Jerusalem, 1953) 1,2ff, as quoted in L. Silberman, "Prophets/Angels, 91.

41. A. Bandstra, "The Law and Angels: Antiquities 15.136 and Galatians 3:19," *CTJ* 24 (1989): 229.

42. Ibid., 230.

Targum Onqelos Deut 33:2

He said, "The Lord revealed Himself from Sinai, the splendor of His glory appeared to us from Seir; He revealed Himself through His power on Mount Paran, and with Him were myriads of holy ones; from the midst of the fire He gave the Law, written by His hand."

Jewish angelology of the Second Temple period partially accounts for variants in versions of Deut 33:2. In the case of Targum Onkelos, B. Grossfeld notes that קְדֶשׁ מֵרְבְבֹת is rendered literally and "so also the Syr, as well as the Pal Tgs.—Ps-Jon., Neof. and the Frg. Tg. (P, V), only the latter specifying 'holy angels' instead of 'holy ones.'"[43] Although most of the Targumic material fails to refer to angels explicitly, the Frg. Tg. (P,V) demonstrate the prominence of the motif of the law mediated by angels by the first centuries CE.

The biblical texts of Deut 33:2 and Ps 68:17 imply that the *elohim*, the sons of God, and the holy ones are God's assemblies of angels who are present on Mt. Sinai at the giving of the law. In fact, Psalm 68 specifically connects the angelic host at Mt. Zion with those at Mt. Sinai.[44] Although Scripture may imply that angels were present on Mt. Sinai at the giving of the Law, the biblical text by itself does not mention what they were doing there.

Due to the fact that angels serve as messengers throughout the Scriptures, it could easily be extrapolated that their presence at Mt. Sinai suggested similar activity. This inference provided a starting point for later interpreters. As a result, the lack of explicit scriptural evidence to support angelic mediation at Sinai is expanded upon in later depictions of Moses' ascent.[45] H. Thackeray, in agreement with Westcott, states, "The passive attendance of angels on Sinai which arose out of Deut 33:2 was then 'by a natural process of interpretation taken to indicate their ministration.'"[46]

Philo does not mention angelic activity at the giving of the Law, yet in *De Somniis* explains the role of angelic mediators:

(141) Now philosophers in general are wont to call these demons, but the sacred scripture calls them angels, using a name more in accordance

---

43. Bernard Grossfeld, trans. and ed., *The Targum Onqelos to Deuteronomy*, vol. 9 of *The Aramaic Bible* (Wilmington: Michael Glazier, Inc., 1988).

44. See, Ps 68:18, רֶכֶב אֱלֹהִים רִבֹּתַיִם אַלְפֵי שִׁנְאָן אֲדֹנָי בָם סִינַי בַּקֹּדֶשׁ

45. Kugel, 247–70. Kugel's second hermeneutical principle is "Exegetical motifs generally arise out of only one focus or site, usually a troubling or suggestive word or phrase within a specific verse."

46. Henry St. John Thackeray, *The Relation of St. Paul to Contemporary Jewish Thought* (New York: The Macmillan Company, 1900), 162.

with nature. For indeed they do report the injunctions of the father to his children and the necessities of the children to the father. (142) And it is in reference to this employment of theirs that the holy scripture has represented them as ascending and descending, not because God, who knows everything before any other being, mediator and intercessor; because of our standing in awe of and fearing the Ruler of the universe, and the all-powerful might of his authority; (143) having received a notion of which he once entreated one of those mediators, saying: 'Do thou speak for us, and let not God speak to us, lest we die.' For not only are we unable to endure his chastisements, but we cannot bear even his excessive and unmodified benefits, which he himself proffers us of his own accord, without employing the ministrations of any other beings."[47]

Another work from the milieu of the first century is Pseudo-Philo (*Liber Antinquitatum Biblicarum*). Like the Septuagint, Pseudo-Philo emphasizes angelic presence at the giving of the Law:

And behold the mountains burned with fire, and the earth quaked, and the hills were disturbed, and the mountains were rolled about, and the abysses boiled, and every habitable place was shaken, and the heavens were folded up, and the clouds drew up water, and flames of fire burned, and thunderings and lightnings were many, and winds and storms roared, the stars gathered together, and *angels* ran on ahead, until God should establish the *Law* of his eternal covenant with the sons of Israel and give his eternal commandments that will not pass away.... And now you were like a flock before our LORD, and he led you into the height of the clouds and set the *angels* beneath your feet and established for you the *Law* and commanded you through the prophets and corrected you through the leaders and showed you not a few wonders . . ."[48] (emphasis added)

Pseudo-Philo accepts the explicit reading of Deut 32:2 and the undesignated role for angels in its portrayal of Moses' ascent.

Other uses of the motif of the law mediated by angels further clarify its development. Terrance Callan summarizes one source's depiction of angelic activity at Moses' ascent:

Jubilees is presented as something spoken by God to Moses on Sinai at the time Moses went up to receive the law. Angels play a prominent part throughout. God directs the angel of the presence to write the history

---

47. *De Somniis* 1:141–43. The reference to Ex 20:19 alludes to the mediatorship of Moses.

48. *Pseudo-Philo* 11:2–3, 5; 30:5.

for Moses (1:27), and the angel begins dictating it to Moses (2:1). In the course of the dictation the angel several times refers to what he has written for Moses in the law (6:22; 30:12, 21; 50:6, 13), presumably referring to the Pentateuch.[49]

Further testimony to the motif from pseudographical literature is described by J.P. Schultz:

> The author of 3 Enoch relates how God revealed to Enoch-Metatron 'the mysteries of Tora . . . and all the depths of the perfect Law . . . and all the secrets of the universe and all the secrets of creation . . .' Enoch-Metatron in turn reveals to Moses these mysteries as well as 'the Gnosis of things above and the fear of heaven.'[50]

Some of the most debated references to the motif of the law mediated by angels occur in the New Testament. What appears to be a united testimony to the motif in Acts 7:38, 53, Gal 3:19 and Heb 2:2 is questioned. The first NT witness to the motif of the law mediated by angels is located in Stephen's speech before the Jerusalem Council.

Acts 7:53

οἵ τινες ἐλάβετε τὸν νόμον εἰς διαταγὰς ἀγγέλων καὶ οὐκ ἐφυλάξατε.

You are the ones that received the law as ordained by angels, and yet you have not kept it.[51]

Stephen's speech makes three additional references to angels:

> Now when forty years had passed, an angel appeared to him in the wilderness of Mount Sinai, in the flame of a burning bush (Acts 7:30).

> It was this Moses whom they rejected when they said, 'Who made you a ruler and a judge?' and whom God now sent as both ruler and liberator through the angel who appeared to him in the bush (Acts 7:35).

> He is the one who was in the congregation in the wilderness with the angel who spoke to him at Mount Sinai, and with our ancestors; and he received living oracles to give to us (Acts 7:38).

---

49. Terrance Callan, "Pauline Midrash: The Exegetical Background of Gal 3:19b," *JBL* 99 (1980): 552–53.

50. J.P. Schultz, "Angelic Opposition to the Ascension of Moses and Revelation of the Law," *JQR* 61 (1971): 296.

51. NT citations are taken from *NRSV* unless otherwise noted.

Both Acts 7:30 and Acts 7:35 refer to 'the angel who appeared to him in the thorn bush.' Then Stephen, in Acts 7:38, appears to associate the angel in the bush with the angel on Mount Sinai. The one 'who appeared to him in the thorn bush' (Acts 7:35) is the angel 'who spoke to him [Moses] on Mount Sinai' (Acts 7:38).[52] The depiction of a single angel speaking to Moses on Sinai is found only in Acts 7:38 in the NT. The allusion to a single angel is likely derived from a pre-existing tradition which adapted the motif of the law mediated by angels.[53] For example, *Apoc. Mos.* refers to an angel on Sinai:

> This is the history and the life of the first-created Adam and Eve. It was revealed by God to his servant Moses when he received the tables of the law from the hand of the Lord. It was transmitted to him by the archangel Michael.

Thus, in Acts 7, the motif includes both the 'singular angel' tradition (7:38) as well as the 'plurality of angels' tradition (7:53).

Although the use of the motif in Acts 7:53 has a more positive connotation than the other NT references, the implied contrast with 'the coming of the Righteous One' is shared by all three occurrences. Acts 7:53, Gal 3:19, and Heb 2:2 seem to cast a shadow on the role of angels in mediating the law in contrast with the epochal coming of a unique messianic mediator.

Galatians 3:19

Τί οὖν ὁ νόμος; τῶν παραβάσεων χάριν προσετέθη, ἄχρις οὗ ἔλθη τὸ σπέρμα ᾧ ἐπήγγελται, διαταγεὶς δι' ἀγγέλων ἐν χειρὶ μεσίτου.

> Why then the law? It was added because of transgressions, until the offspring would come to whom the promise had been made; and it was ordained through angels by a mediator.

---

52. Acts 7:38 may refer back to LXX Deuteronomy 33:2, Acts 7:30 to Exodus 3:2, and Acts 7:35 to Exodus 14:19. Acts departs from the LXX by omitting κυρίου from LXX Exodus 3:2 which has ἄγγελος κυρίου. Usually, Acts stays close to the LXX as Johnson notes, "In no place does he distort the text of the Septuagint; in fact in most places he uses the very words of Scripture" (Luke Timothy Johnson, *The Acts of the Apostles*, vol. 5 of *Sacra Pagina Series*, ed. Daniel J. Harrington (Collegeville, MN: The Liturgical Press, 1992), 137).

53. The inclusion of this distinct form of the motif from earlier texts is not surprising. Acts is known to have repeatedly relied on pseudographical traditions. Cf. the allusions in Acts 7:23, 30 to Jubilees 47:10; 48:2.

Gal 3:19 is set in the context of contrasting covenants. In Galatians 3:15–22 the word covenant is used twice[54] and Gal 4:21–31 provides further discussion of the δύο διαθῆκαι.[55] These two covenants are identified in Galatians 3 as the Mosaic covenant, which is 'based on law' and the Abrahamic covenant, which is 'by means of a promise.'[56] Paul gives a purpose of the Law, which may be considered more broadly the Mosaic covenant.[57] He states, "Why the Law then? It was added because of transgressions, having been ordained[58] through angels by the agency of a mediator, until the seed should come to whom the promise had been made."[59]

T. Callan captures the midrashic argument of Gal 3:19–20:

> Paul uses the tension between the way the law was given and the oneness
> of God to support his contention that the law was a temporary measure
> for the sake of transgression, but he stops short of denying that it comes
> from God. That Paul here points to a tension between the giving of the law
> and the oneness of God receives some confirmation from his emphasis
> elsewhere in Gal 3 on the oneness of the messiah. The messiah is the one
> seed of Abraham (v 16) in whom all are made one (v 28). Thus the messiah
> conforms to the oneness of God as the mediation of the law does not.[60]

While dependent on Jewish thought and method, Paul draws on a distinctly Jewish motif, i.e., the law mediated by angels. H. Riesenfeld captures Paul's use of the motif:

> Taking advantage of two ideas which were commonly accepted in con-
> temporary Judaism, the role of the angels at the giving of the Law and the
> superiority of oneness to plurality, he manages to prove that the Law is

---

54. Gal 3:15, 17.

55. Gal 4:24.

56. Gal 3:18.

57. The polyvalency of νόμος has received attention from D.J. Moo, "'Law,' 'Works of the Law,' and Legalism in Paul," *WTJ* 45 (1983): 73–100. Moo designates nine uses of νόμος by Paul, and Galatians 3:19b falls under the usage labeled a system or an economy. He holds, "What is vital for any accurate understanding of Paul's doctrine of law is to realize that Paul uses *nomos* most often and most basically of the Mosaic law" (80).

58. H.N. Ridderbos, *The Epistle of Paul to the Churches of Galatia* (Grand Rapids: Eerdmans, 1953), 139. Ridderbos notes that διατάσσειν "is a technical term for the carrying out of laws and ordinances." See also 1 Cor 7:17; 9:14; 11:34; 16:1; Tit 1:5.

59. Gal 3:19

60. T. Callan, "Pauline Midrash: The Exegetical Background of Gal 3:19b," *Journal of Biblical Literature* 99 (1980): 565.

inferior to the promise. . . . Thus Paul repudiates his adversaries by means of conceptions which they had previously accepted.[61]

Hebrews 2:2

εἰ γὰρ ὁ δι᾽ ἀγγέλων λαληθεὶς λόγος ἐγένετο βέβαιος καὶ πᾶσα παράβασις καὶ παρακοὴ ἔλαβεν ἔνδικον μισθαποδοσίαν . . .

For if the message declared through angels was valid, and every transgression or disobedience received a just penalty . . .

Angelic mediators are a major issue in Hebrews 1–2. The issue warrants seven citations from the Hebrew Bible that are used to substantiate the superiority of Jesus to the angels.[62] In addition to dependence on Scripture, the writer makes his case through the motif of the law mediated by angels. Although the presence of the motif in the NT is perspicuous, R. Nash holds to a hypothetical view of the motif. Nash states,

> The writer like Paul in Gal. 3:19 was referring to a current Jewish belief that the angels had played a role when the Law was given through Moses (see Acts 7:53). There is no reason to believe either writer was necessarily endorsing this belief which appears to lack any Old Testament support. The argument in both Heb. 2:2 and Gal. 3:19 can be viewed as hypothetical. That is, even if angels did play a role in the mediation of the Law, consider how much greater is the Gospel and its Mediator.[63]

The support that Nash garners for this view is "the writer of Hebrews will have nothing to do with the multiple mediators of the Alexandrians."[64] Yet, at the same time, Nash weakens his position by establishing the Alexandrian background of Hebrews and by noting Hebrew's affinities to Philonic thought.[65] While the writer of

61. H. Riesenfeld, "The Misinterpreted Mediator in Gal 3:19–20," *The New Testament Age* 2 (1984): 409.

62. R. Nash, "The Notion of Mediator in Alexandrian Judaism and the Epistle to the Hebrews," *Westminster Theological Journal* 40 (Fall 1977–Spring 1978): 89–115. Nash notes, "These quotations are used to make three main points: (a) Christ is God the Son whom angels must worship (1:5–6); (b) Christ is the King whom the angels must obey (1:7–9); (c) Christ is God the Creator whom the angels must serve (1:10–12)."

63. Ibid., 11.

64. Ibid.

65. Ibid., 92–100. Nash gives five arguments for Hebrew's Alexandrian background: "1. Hebrews contains an implicit Wisdom-Christology that has affinities to the Alexandrian teaching about Sophia.

Hebrews warns against the dangers of Philonic influence in certain cases, this well-established motif is at home in the context of Alexandrian Judaism. Furthermore, the εἰ of Hebrews 2:2 has the sense of "since" which argues against the hypothetical view.

The view of angels as prophets surfaces again with an alternative reading of Hebrews 2:2. L. Silberman proposes that LXX's reading, *angelon autou*, which may be a translation of a reading in 11QPSa 151 (*nby'w*), reflects a tradition that is also witnessed in the NT. He comments, "May it not be that the occurrence of *tois prophetais* in Heb 1,2 and of *angelon* in 2,2 to designate the "mediators" between God and Israel reflect this tradition?"[66] However, both the infrequency of prophets being designated angels and the NT contexts mitigate against Silberman's position.

Hebrews also accepts another motif associated with heavenly ascent, i.e., the angelic assembly. The earthly assembly is presented as fellowshipping and worshipping with 'myriads of angels'.[67] This conjoined earthly and heavenly assemblies shift location from Mt. Sinai (Heb 2:2) to Mt. Zion (Heb 12:22). [68]

By the Rabbinic period, the motif of the law mediated by angels experienced resistance in rabbinic quarters due to an anti-apocalyptic motive and the possible influence of a developing anti-Christian polemic. W.D. Davies summarizes the rabbinic material in connection with this motif:

> Some [rabbinic] passages suggest that after the close of the New Testament period efforts were made in some quarters to belittle the role of the angels on Mt. Sinai. In Deut. R. 7:9 Yahweh refused to give the Torah to the ministering angels though they coveted it. In Deut. R. 8:2 the ministering angels eagerly desired the Torah, it is claimed, but it was too abstruse for them. According to other passages Moses had, metaphorically, to wrestle with the angels on Mt. Sinai: they pleaded that man was unworthy of the Torah, and wanted it for themselves (See Exod. R. 28:I; Shabb. 88b.). In Song of Songs R. I:2 R. Johanan's view that angels mediated between Yahweh and the Israelites at Sinai is expressly set over against that of the Rabbis who insisted that it was each commandment itself which went in turn to each

---

... 2. Hebrews contains an implicit Logos-Christology similar to the Alexandrian Logos doctrine. . . . 3. Hebrews assigns mediatorial functions to Jesus that are similar to the functions of Alexandrian mediators. . . . 4. Hebrews asserts the superiority of Jesus over a group of individuals and classes that served mediatorial functions in Alexandrian thought. . . . 5. The Epistle to the Hebrews manifests a Platonic distinction between a shadowy and less perfect earthly temple and the perfect heavenly temple.

66. L. Silberman, "Prophets/Angels," 92.

67. Cf. 1 Cor 11:10, 'because of the angels.'

68. Cf. Heb 12:25 and Hebrews 2:2.

of the Israelites not an angel mediating a commandment. It will be recalled that in a passage near to the first two cited above, i.e., Deut. R. 8:6 there is probably anti-Christian polemic . . . .[69]

T. Callan also highlights the range of rabbinic understanding of angels in relation to the Law:

> In a series of rabbinic interpretations dating from the 2nd and 3rd centuries, these angels are variously understood as the angelic princes of the peoples of the world [*Pesiq. R.* 21.8], or as ones present to destroy those who would not accept the law [*Pesiq. Rab Kah.* 12.22], or to help Israel to endure the giving of the law [*Mek. Bahodesh* 9], or to honor the Torah or Israel for accepting it [*Pesiq. R.* 21.8], or as ones who opposed God's giving the law to Moses [*Pesiq. R.* 20.4].[70]

Two other rabbinic witnesses accept the presence of angels on Sinai, yet fall short of recognizing angels as mediators of the law:

> When the Holy One revealed Himself on Mount Sinai, twenty-two thousand angels descended on Him, as it is written, "God's chariot [includes] twice ten thousand, thousands of angels" (Tehillim 68.18).

> Rebbi said: "On the day that the Holy One descended upon Mount Sinai to give the Torah to Israel, six hundred thousand angels descended with Him, and in the hand of each one was a crown for Israel" (Shir ha-Shirim 4).[71]

Although the rabbinic testimony to the motif of the law mediated by angels is one-sided in its resistance, at least two witnesses accept the motif:

> Thus it was found written in a text brought out of the Diaspora: Two myriads of angels of the kind known as *''Ife sine'an* came down with the Holy One, blessed be He, on Mount Sinai to give the Torah to Israel. *(Pesiq. R.* 21.8)

> An angel would bring forth each of the words from the divine presence and carry it around to each individual Israelite asking, 'do you accept this word? Thus and so are the decreed implicit in it . . .' To which each Israelite would respond, Yea!! Immediately he kissed him upon his mouth as it is

69. W.D. Davies, "A Note on Josephus, Antiquities 15:136," *HTR* 97 (1954): 140.

70. T. Callan, "*Pauline Midrash*," 551–552.

71. Schlomo Rozner, *A Nation of Witnesses* (Jerusalem: Feldheim Publishers, 1996), 79.

written: 'to you was it shown that you might know' (Deut 4,35) by a mes-
senger. (*Midrash Song of Songs Rabbah* 1.2)

In the midst of significant resistance to the motif in rabbinic literature, vestiges of
the motif are preserved. Even so, a few scholars have denied the presence of the
motif in Jewish literature.[72] However, a closer look at the motif's underlying social
forces demonstrates its appropriateness during the Second Temple Period.

During periods in which greater emphasis was placed on the transcendence
of God, biblical texts were reinterpreted. The Second Temple Period marked such a
shift in Jewish interpreters' view of God's transcendence. J.H. Charlesworth states,

> Most pseudepigrapha, in contrast to early Jewish writings, are character-
> ized by an increasing claim that God is thoroughly majestic and transcen-
> dent (2Mac 3:39; 3Mac 2:15; SibOr 3:1, 11, 81, 807; 5.298, 352; MartIs
> 1:6b; 1En 71:5–11; 2En 20:5).[73]

In order to compensate for the increased transcendence of God, the activity of
angels increased.[74] Angels become more intimately involved in the human realm.
The interchangeability of angels with the presence and activity of God provided a
bridge for the ever-widening gulf between God and humanity.[75] For example, the
joining of the earthly assembly with the heavenly assembly appears numerous times
in Scripture and in the literature of Qumran.[76] In this social context, it was a natural
assumption that the angels, the quintessential mediators between God and humanity, participated in the giving of the Law. The acceptance of the motif became one
way of emphasizing mediators in Second Temple literature. While the motif could
have been resisted during this period, an emphasis on angelic activity drove its acceptance and inclusion.

Heavenly ascent motifs have taken various paths and operated distinctly in
manifold contexts. As for the motif of the law mediated by angels, examples were
given that demonstrated the motif's acceptance, resistance, and emphasis in a vari-

72. See note 3.

73. J.H. Charlesworth, *The Old Testament Pseudepigrapha*, vol. 2 (Garden City: Doubleday, 1983),
xxxi.

74. One example of this phenomenon is Jubilees, a second-century BCE work that delineates eight
types of angels.

75. Scripture already contained a launching pad for the development. See Gen 1:26; 32:1–2; 48:15–
18; Ex 13:21; 14:19.

76. See Job 1:6; Ps 82:1; 1 Kgs 22:19; Dan 7:10; 1QS 2:25; 1QS 11:7–9; 1QH 3:21; 1QH 11:11, 12.

ety of social settings and texts. As such, the motif provides a clear example of a motif subject to semantic accent.

The substantial use of the motif also bears witness to its prominence and the interdependence of the sources. In most cases, the motif's acceptance, emphasis, or resistance in the LXX, Pseudepigrapha and Apocrypha, NT, and rabbinic writings was based on prior use and the contemporary author's polemic. Although this essay offers a close look at the trajectory of one motif, further work remains to be done which examines all the motifs associated with Moses' ascents.

ANDREW SPARKS (M.Div., S.T.M., M.B.A.) has served the Messianic Jewish community for more than fifteen years in a variety of capacities including as Editor in Chief for *Kesher*. He also serves as Chief Advancement Officer and Chief Operating Officer of Messianic Jewish Theological Institute.

Gentile Yeshua-Believers Praying in the Synagogue: Why and How

Jon C. Olson

Introduction

I have been praying in the synagogue for more than twenty-five years—yet I am not Jewish. This essay explains in both theoretical and practical terms how and why Gentile Yeshua-believers may pray the traditional Jewish liturgy in the company of Jews.

It is with a measure of trepidation that I discuss how Jewish and Gentile believers might worship together, using Jewish forms. First, I have a serious concern about Christian theological anti-Judaism, including supersessionism, and anxiety about how my essay might be used.[1] Second, I have a personal stake in how non-Yeshua-believing Jews react (though this essay is not written to them), because I pray in their midst.

My argument is directed to Yeshua-believing Gentiles without ignoring Yeshua-believing Jews. I argue that it is important for Gentiles to both identify with, and distinguish themselves from, Jews in prayer. By establishing clear boundaries, more freedom within the boundaries becomes possible.

The foundation, the "why" for Gentile Yeshua-believers to pray the traditional Jewish liturgy in the company of Jews, may be sketched as follows. First, God has elected the descendants of Abraham, Isaac, and Jacob, and made a covenant with the Jewish people that continues today. Second, the Torah and its practices are a part of God's covenant with the Jewish people. Third, the worship practices transmitted by rabbinic Judaism, and rooted in the Torah, are a means of preserving the Jewish people, and are usable by Yeshua-believers. Fourth, the church participates through

---

1. Jonathan Kaplan writes, "we must be careful not to engage in a hermeneutic of promise-fulfillment where we merely show how the expectations of redemption present in the prayer book are fulfilled in Yeshua. Such a practice does violence to the liturgy and sustains a supersessionist polemic to the detriment of our community" (Jonathan Kaplan, "A Divine Tapestry—Reading the Siddur, Reading Redemption, Reading Yeshua," 45 [Hashivenu Forum 2004]).

Yeshua in Israel's covenantal privileges.[2] Fifth, Gentiles who come to faith in Yeshua are not required to convert to Judaism nor to assume the commandments uniquely given to Jews. Sixth, the social expression of the gospel is reconciliation among peoples who are, and who remain, different.[3]

Personal Background

I am a Christian who since 1982 has used the traditional *siddur* (Jewish prayer book) in worship services at Orthodox synagogues and in my prayers at home. I am well-received in most Orthodox synagogues. I tell the synagogue's rabbi who I am. I come in order to pray, and am fluent in the prayers.

I also pray in a Messianic synagogue[4] and in Christian worship services. My wife often joins me in these settings. Participating in the life of several religious communities has both blessings and drawbacks.

Although I once seriously thought of converting to Judaism, I feel that I can serve God better without becoming a Jew. Some years after reaching that decision, I joined a Mennonite congregation through baptism and confession of faith. Mennonite identity is important to me. Mennonites are rare where I now live, so this takes all the more effort.

In conversations prior to baptism, I related my intention to continue attending services in an Orthodox synagogue. I drew upon historical and theological writings concerning the relations of Jews and Christians, the church as social embodiment, and the relationship of one's social location to one's interpretation of the Bible. I agree with Willard Swartley, who wrote:

> Test your co-creative experience of interpretation with brothers and sisters in the believing community, and perhaps also with some unbelievers. The purpose of the testing is not merely to ascertain whether a particular understanding is correct or appropriate, but to make one's own life-world a part of a corporate life-world and thus contribute to the reality of Christian (or Jewish) community, fulfilling the edificatory function of Scripture.[5]

2. See Rom 11; Eph 2; 1 Pet 2.

3. See Mark Thiessen Nation, *John Howard Yoder: Mennonite Patience, Evangelical Witness, Catholic Convictions* (Grand Rapids: Eerdmans, 2006), 120, discussing Yoder's *The Politics of Jesus*.

4. Congregation Shuvah Yisrael (Bloomfield, CT) led by Rabbi Paul Saal.

5. Willard Swartley, *Slavery, Sabbath, War & Women: Case Issues in Biblical Interpretation* (Scottdale: Herald Press, 1983), 227. See also Richard B. Hays, "The Church as Embodied Metaphor," in *The Moral Vision of the New Testament* (San Francisco: HarperSanFrancisco, 1996). Mark Kinzer,

Richard B. Hays also wrote:

> Under the guidance of the Spirit, we discover the operation of God's grace among us to be prefigured in Scripture, and we find the Scripture that we thought we knew transfigured by the grace at work among us.[6]

When I began attending a Messianic synagogue, I decided to continue worshipping at an Orthodox synagogue. (I alternate between them on Saturday mornings.) I had already developed a habit of reading large portions of the traditional prayers when I decided not to convert to Judaism. Therefore, I evaluate many Hebrew prayers, not with the question of whether to start praying them, but with the question of whether to continue praying them.

Love and Hate for Things Jewish Among Gentile Believers

In an essay about Karl Barth, Michael Wyschogrod concludes: "I have said that it is for gentiles to love Israel. This, of course, is wrong, it cannot be asked of gentiles. But it can be asked of Christians."[7] Wyschogrod and others recognize the special theological affinity of Christians for Jews. "The God of Israel is not separable from the people of Israel. It follows that to be in relationship with the God of Israel is to be in relationship with the people of Israel."[8] Knowledge of Judaism is essential for Christians who wish to understand their faith. As Wyschogrod put it, "the loyalty to the scriptural is therefore a spiritual conversion to Israel's mind."[9]

In the ancient Roman world, Gentile God-fearers were present in synagogues and were a source of many early Christian converts. Paula Fredricksen remarks that "there is no reason to think that Paul's gentiles, now that they've made the incred-

---

in *Postmissionary Messianic Judaism*, 46, writes that competing interpretative schemes should be influenced by "(1) recognition that the social location of the authors and initial readers of the text (all part of the Jewish movement) was dramatically different from our own (boxed into mutually exclusive Jewish and Christian categories and social worlds); (2) examination of the ethical implications of each interpretive scheme, as seen in the histories of those who have adopted them; (3) reflection on the theological implications of important historical developments in the life of the Jewish people in relation to the church."

6. Richard B. Hays, *Echoes of Scripture in the Letters of Paul* (New Haven: Yale, 1989), 184.

7. Michael Wyschogrod, "Why Was and Is the Theology of Karl Barth of Interest to a Jewish Theologian?" in *Abraham's Promise* (Grand Rapids: Eerdmans, 2004), 224.

8. Richard John Neuhaus, "Salvation is from the Jews," in *Jews and Christians*, ed. Carl E. Braaten and Robert W. Jenson (Grand Rapids: Eerdmans, 2003), 68.

9. Wyschogrod, *Abraham's Promise*, 216.

ible commitment to the God of Israel by not worshipping their own gods anymore, would stop going to the synagogue and listening to the Bible."[10] Judaism was popular enough that Juvenal satirized Roman citizens for keeping the Sabbath, food laws, and other Jewish practices. Centuries later, John Chrysostom gave sermons against Christians attending both church and synagogue, providing evidence for the popularity of the practice. Chrysostom and others dissuaded Christians from praying with Jews by outlawing the practice and by espousing a teaching of contempt for Jews and Judaism. This teaching has in recent years been repudiated by the Roman Catholic church and several Protestant bodies,[11] yet much estrangement still exists.

Identity, Boundaries, and Estrangement

Marc Gopin has suggested that it is not boundaries that create conflict, but the interpretation of the boundaries. He believes that all people need to feel unique as well as to integrate with others. An inappropriate response to these needs is to couple group solidarity with a view of strangers characterized by fear, hatred or indifference. As a biblical corrective, Gopin notes that the stranger (*ger*) is to be included in celebrations of the faith community.[12]

Abraham is the quintessential stranger in his self-perception and in his embrace of the unknown other. Abraham introduced himself to the residents of Canaan with the words, "I am a stranger and a resident among you" (Gen 23:4). Abraham's definition of his dual status describes the historical position of the Jew who resides in a predominantly non-Jewish society.[13] Countless people are now living away from their land of origin, and the Abrahamic story gives meaning to their situation. The key is how we negotiate the boundaries with the stranger. Moreover, the stranger

10. "Paul and Paula," Interview of Paula Fredricksen with David Hulme, *Vision* (Fall 2005). Online: http://www.vision.org/visionmedia/article.aspx?id=144&terms=paul+and+paula.

11. Helga Croner, ed., *Stepping Stones to Further Jewish-Christian Relations: An Unabridged Collection of Christian Documents* (London: Stimulus Books, 1973); Helga Croner, ed., *More Stepping Stones to Jewish-Christian Relations* (New York: Paulist Press, 1985); John T. Pawlikowski, "Reflections on Covenant and Mission: Forty Years After Nostra Aetate," *Cross Currents* (Winter 2007). Online: http://www.crosscurrents.org/Pawlikowski0406.htm.

12. Marc Gopin, *Between Eden and Armageddon: The Future of World Religions, Violence, and Peacemaking* (New York: Oxford University Press, 2000), 3–5. Cf. Jon C. Olson, "Which Differences are Blessed? From Peter's Vision to Paul's Letters," *Journal of Ecumenical Studies* 37:3–4 (2000): 455–60.

13. Abraham Besdin, *Reflections of the Rav: Lessons in Jewish Thought adapted from the lectures of Rabbi Joseph B. Soloveitchik* (Jerusalem: Department for Torah Education and Culture in the Diaspora of the World Zionist Organization, 1979), 169–77.

may turn out to be kin. The heart of Gopin's peacemaking is the mythic recovery of the "lost brother," for Jews, Christians, and Muslims all trace themselves to Abraham in one way or another.[14]

The estrangement of Jews and Gentiles in the people of God is similar to the "failure in peoplehood" of whites and blacks in the American church. James McClendon argues that, extending from the time of American slavery, blacks and whites have had different hermeneutics, cultures, and church discipline.[15]

Both corporate and individual response to this estrangement of peoples may be appropriate.

> The emergence of "one new humanity" in this case is not to be assumed as a cost-free outcome of Christians' good intentions. Rather than 'integration'... a valuable first step is crossing over, that is, the deliberate choice of some from each people to connect with a congregation of the other people. This crossing over need not be for a lifetime, and it will not be without its distinct joys. . . . [16]

Glen Stassen and David Gushee add that white Christians, in part due to an individualistic understanding of sin and salvation, are often unwilling or unable to recognize the social dimensions of race relations. Racial justice, rather than racial reconciliation, should be the American church's primary paradigm about race.[17]

My analogy between black-white relations and Jewish-Christian relations suggests that Christianity and Judaism are different cultures, that some individual crossing over may be appropriate, and that justice may be a more appropriate paradigm than reconciliation.[18]

14. Marc Gopin, *Holy War, Holy Peace: How Religion Can Bring Peace to the Middle East* (New York: Oxford University Press, 2002), 33. Cf., Jon Olson, (review) *Holy War, Holy Peace Kesher* 16 (Fall 2003), 146–58. In Isaiah 57:19, "Peace, peace, to the far and the near," the far are those Jews who were taken into exile, the near those left at home in Judah. Ephesians 2:12–13 uses the Isaiah passage to reclassify Gentiles as those who were exiles and far. "The proclamation of peace to the far becomes thus a search for alienated and lost family members—for 'us away from home.'" [Tom Yoder Neufeld, "'For he is our peace' Ephesians 2:11–22," in Mary H. Schertz and Ivan Friesen, eds., *Beautiful Upon the Mountains: Biblical Essays on Mission, Peace, and the Reign of God* (Elkhart, IN: Institute of Mennonite Studies, 2003), 227.

15. James McClendon, *Witness: Systematic Theology* (Nashville: Abingdon, 2000), 375.

16. McClendon, *Witness*, 378. For reflections about crossing over, see John Paul Lederach, *The Moral Imagination: The Art and Soul of Building Peace* (New York: Oxford University Press, 2005).

17. Glenn H. Stassen and David P. Gushee, *Kingdom Ethics: Following Jesus and Contemporary Context* (Downers Grove: Intervarsity, 2003), 406.

18. Cf. John H. Yoder, *The Jewish-Christian Schism Revisited*, Michael G. Cartwright and Peter Ochs,

Rich Nichol has written that "identity confusion has been the hallmark of Messianic Judaism."[19] While Gentiles are not required to observe all the commandments that Jews do (Acts 15:28–29), they may desire in synagogue worship to observe as many as possible. In Messianic Judaism, Jews are rarely perceived as having onerous tasks which Gentiles would gladly avoid.[20] Rather, any differences are perceived as privileges from which Gentiles are excluded.[21]

Torah Observance among Jewish Believers in Yeshua

Mark Kinzer has made the case for Torah observance and respect for rabbinic tradition by Jews within the body of Messiah:[22]

> It is not the particular manner of Torah observance practiced by Yeshua and his followers that is authoritative for us, but *the fact* that they saw the basics of such practice as a divinely mandated covenantal duty, and *the*

eds. (Grand Rapids: Eerdmans, 2003), 265 (Appendix B). A model for Jewish-Christian reconciliation (with diaconal service; Rom 15:27) is provided by the Nes Ammim community in northern Israel. A positive model for Messianic Jewish interaction with various groups is Keren HaShlichut in Jerusalem (http://www.shlichut.com).

19. Richard C. Nichol, "The Case for Conversion: Welcoming Non-Jews into Messianic Jewish Space," *Kesher* 19 (Summer 2005): 10.

20. This perception might change if more of the onerous (fasting) or countercultural (no Sabbath driving) Jewish practices are adopted within Messianic Judaism. Still, religions that make demands upon adherents are also appealing.

21. Paul Saal ("Toward a Messianic Moral Vision," Hashivenu Forum 2005, 20) writes "of the difficulty in drawing boundaries when mediating between equality and sameness, and … the emotional response that is elicited when inviting people only part way into the family." Douglas Harink ("Celebrating the Gentiles Among You: A Response to Richard Nichol," *Kesher* 19 [Summer 2005]: 82–83) writes, "The practice of Judaism is a participation in an identity that is historically rich, tested by fire, ritually thick, and spiritually satisfying. Given the thin and unbearably light identities typically mediated by postmodern, late-capitalist, consumerist, American culture, it is no wonder that the encounter with a cultural identity bearing the substance and weight of Judaism leads Gentile believers to want to identify with all things "Jewish" (as they see them)." Mark Nanos ("Rethinking the 'Paul *and* Judaism' Paradigm: Why Not 'Paul's Judaism?'" 35) writes of the apostle's view, "Non-Jews were not under Torah; they were nevertheless obliged to observe the appropriate halakhah for this association as equals to take place. That is an idealistic notion within the constraints of the present age, when discrimination ineluctably accompanies difference. But Paul believed the age to come had dawned, changing the terms, so that discrimination was to be eliminated by way of living according to the Spirit, that is, according to the age-to-come-way-of-life the Spirit made possible within this community, if they will dedicate themselves to walking in the Spirit."

22. Kinzer, *Postmissionary Messianic Judaism*. See also responses in *Kesher* 20 (2006) and *Mishkan* 48 (2006); *Pro Ecclesia* 16:1 (2007); Mark Kinzer, "Post-Missionary Messianic Judaism Three Years Later" (2008), online: www.mjti.com.

> *way* they engaged with the various attempts to embody such practice that
> had developed among the Jews of their time....[23]

Kinzer summarizes evidence in Matthew, Luke, and Paul for a theological motive underlying the Torah observance of first-century Jewish Yeshua-believers.[24]

The Gospel of Matthew presents Yeshua the Torah teacher as distinguishing between greater/heavier and lesser/lighter commandments (Matt 5:19). The former take precedence over the latter when obligations conflict with one another; however, the lesser/lighter commandments remain authoritative as divine directives to the Jewish people. This means that Jewish practices such as Sabbath, dietary laws, and circumcision are indispensable, enduring elements within the Torah.

The Gospel of Luke begins with two pairs of devout, Torah-observant families: Zechariah and Elizabeth (and their son, John), and Joseph and Miriam (and their son, Yeshua). The first pair lived "blamelessly according to all the commandments and regulations of the Lord (Luke 1:6), while the second pair did "everything required by the Torah of the Lord" (Luke 2:39). The book ends as it begins, with a group of faithful Jews caring for the body of Yeshua, but in compliance with traditional Sabbath practice, "according to the commandment" (Luke 23:56). The book of Acts continues in the same way, stating that the Jewish Yeshua-believers in Jerusalem were "all zealous for the Torah" (Acts 21:20).

Paul's teaching about Torah observance has the major premise that all who are circumcised should remain circumcised (i.e. should accept and affirm their circumcision and its implications) (1 Cor 7:17–20). Paul also taught that Gentiles should not seek circumcision or the Torah obligations of Jews (Gal 5:3). Thus, Matthew, Luke, and Paul agree that Torah observance is normative for all Jews, regardless of whether the wider Jewish community is complying with this norm.

"Postbiblical Jewish institutions that had achieved [widespread] acceptance —such as the synagogue with its attendant pattern of public Scripture reading, or the recitation of blessings before eating bread or drinking wine — are received without question by Yeshua, the apostles, and the New Testament authors."[25] Furthermore,

---

23. Mark Kinzer, "Response to Mishkan Reviewers of My Book," *Mishkan* 48 (2006): 59–60.

24. Mark Kinzer, "Rejoinder to Responses to *Postmissionary Messianic Judaism*," *Kesher* 20 (Winter/Spring 2006): 56–64.

25. Kinzer, *Postmissionary Messianic Judaism*, 260. Following the gift of the Holy Spirit at Pentecost, the early church "devoted themselves to the apostles' teaching and fellowship, to the breaking of bread and the prayers" (Acts 2:42 NRSV). Arthur Glasser interprets "the prayers" to mean the liturgical prayers of the synagogue ("Messianic Jews and the German Church Today," *Direction* 28:1 [Spring 1999]: 46–64. Online: http://www.directionjournal.org/article/?1000). Philip Segal proposes that Luke

the Apostolic Council in Jerusalem (Acts 15), which was convened to decide whether Gentiles who turn to Yeshua are obliged to be circumcised and keep the whole Torah, had as its premise that Jewish believers in Yeshua are obligated to observe Torah. It follows that this Torah obligation will often be expressed in characteristically Jewish and biblical forms of prayer.

Basis for Gentile Believers to Identify with Jews in Prayer

Robert Jenson sees in the Incarnation the foundation for an ecclesiology in solidarity with Israel.

> Paul teaches, and the church follows his teaching, that the church is the body of the risen Christ, and Paul does not initially mean that as a trope. As my body is myself as I am present and available to you, so the church is Christ's presence to the world. . . . But what sort of body is this body?
>
> Can there be a present body of the risen Jew, Jesus of Nazareth, in which the lineage of Abraham and Sarah so vanishes into a congregation of gentiles as it does in the church? My final—and perhaps most radical— suggestion to Christian theology . . . is that . . . the embodiment of the risen Christ is whole only in the form of the church and an identifiable community of Abraham and Sarah's descendants. The church and the synagogue are together and only together the present availability to the world of the risen Jesus Christ.[26]

Not only is Yeshua present among the Jewish people who form part of the church, but he is present even among non-Yeshua-believing Israel.

The Tanakh (Hebrew Bible) and Apostolic Writings (New Testament) envision Gentiles praising and praying to God with Israel in the past, present, and future (e.g. Ps 68:31; Zech 8:20–23; Isa 56:3–8; Rom 15:9–12; Rev 7). Markus Barth, based upon the letter to the Ephesians, thought that Jews and Christians ought to pray together.[27] Together, the Torah obligation of all Jews, the presence of Yeshua among the Jewish people, and the expectation that Gentiles will worship God with Jews in the world to come, suggest that Gentile Christians and Gentiles within Messianic Judaism may, as a sign of the new age brought by Yeshua, pray with Jews in Jewish settings.[28]

11:2 ("say this when you pray") means that the disciples are to recite the Lord's Prayer at the conclusion of the Amidah ("Early Christian and Rabbinic Liturgical Affinities," *New Testament Studies* 30 [1984]: 74).

26. Robert W. Jenson, "Toward a Christian Theology of Judaism," in *Jews and Christians*, ed. Carl E. Braaten and Robert W. Jenson (Grand Rapids: Eerdmans, 2003), 12–13..

27. Markus Barth, *The People of God*, JSNT Suppl. Series 5 (Sheffield: JSOT Press, 1983), 65.

28. Markus Barth's argument supports a reciprocity by which Jewish believers should from time to

The apostle Paul wrote to the Gentile believers in Corinth that the Israelites were "our fathers" (1 Cor 10:1). Hays comments:

> It may seem odd that Paul would describe the Israelites this way in a letter addressed to the predominantly Gentile congregation at Corinth, who of course are not the physical descendants of Israel, but Paul's language reveals something essential about his understanding of the church. His Gentile converts, he believes, have been grafted into the covenant people (cf. Rom 11:17–24) in such a way that they belong to Israel (cf. Gal 6:16). Thus, the story of Israel is for the Gentile Corinthians, not somebody else's story; it is the story of their own spiritual ancestors.[29]

Paul did not say that only the biblical heroes of faith were the ancestors of the Corinthian believers, but particularly the generation that displeased God and failed to enter the Promised Land (1 Cor 10:5f). Thus, even if one were to propose that non-Yeshua-believing Jews in their synagogues are "notorious sinners," they would still be spiritual kinsmen with whom Yeshua-believing Gentiles can pray.[30] Based on this identification of Paul's Corinthian converts with the Hebrews whom God led out of Egypt, it seems that Gentiles can say communal Jewish prayers that also name Israelites as "our fathers" and the Israel of all times as "us."

Basis for Gentile Believers to Distinguish Themselves from Jews in Prayer

In Jewish tradition, God relates to non-Jews through his covenant with Noah. A contemporary Noachide movement has sprung up with rabbinic guidance, and a Bnei Noach *siddur* was published in 2007.[31] The rabbinic treatment of Noachides may be instructive for Gentile Yeshua-believers, even though the modern Noachide movement often denigrates belief in Yeshua as a grave sin.

---

time pray with Gentile believers in demonstrably Gentile places of, or forms of, worship. I think this is a good thing to do as long as the activities are not prohibited to, or offensive to, either party. See for example prayer among members of the World Christian Gathering of Indigenous Peoples and Keren HaShlichut.

29. Richard B. Hays, *First Corinthians: A Bible Commentary for Teaching and Preaching* (Louisville: John Knox Press, 1997), 160. See also Robert W. Jenson, "Scripture's Authority in the Church," in Ellen F. Davis and Richard B. Hays, eds., *The Art of Reading Scripture* (Grand Rapids: Eerdmans, 2003), 30.

30. More accurately, they are a holy congregation. I also believe that prayer with non-Yeshua-believing Jews is a safeguard against Christian-based supersessionism.

31. Excerpts from *Service of the Heart: Renewing the Ancient Path of Biblical Prayer and Service* (Rose, OK: OKBNS Press, 2007), are available online: http://www.okbns.org/Free.html.

Noachides consider it good to bless God in daily activities, e.g. before and after eating, when waking and going to sleep, and so on. If a Gentile knows Hebrew, it is good to pray in that language.[32] Some Noachides have tried to create prayers based only on Hebrew prayers that were designed for Israel. However, other Noachides believe that the inaccessibility of Jewish prayer services to Gentiles is part of God's larger plan.[33]

Michael Katz, writing for the Root and Branch Association, states that Bnei Noach may not say "who has sanctified us by his commandments," regarding something that they are not commanded to do, or "who has taken us out of Egypt," nor may they observe the Sabbath and Festivals in the manner that Jews do.[34]

Despite differences between rabbinic Judaism and the apostle Paul regarding the relationship of Gentile believers to Israel, both retain an important principle —namely that Jews and Gentiles need to remain distinct. (For example, Paul opposed the circumcision of Gentile believers, and continued to use the terms "Jew" and "Gentile" within the body of Messiah.) Jew/Gentile distinction is intrinsic to the biblical vision, one of mutual blessing by groups who are and who remain different (Gen 12:3; 1 Cor 12; Gal 3:28–29).[35]

> We remember that Paul's "mystery" is that Jews and Greeks are reconciled and made one in the church. The relationship between husband and wife, therefore, symbolizes the mystery of unity in plurality and makes it present within the community. This completes the Pauline perception of "neither Jew nor Greek, neither male nor female." . . . Man and woman submit to each other in respect and love and service, finding unity and peace not in a false identification but in a pluralistic unity. So should Jew and Greek celebrate their unity in service to each other, so that God's purpose might be fulfilled, "to unite all things in him, things in heaven and things on earth" (Eph. 1:10).[36]

32. Boruch Ellison, "A Universal Prayer Guide for Hasidic Gentiles" (from the *Jews and Hasidic Gentiles United to Save America* website associated with Chabad Lubavitch and combative toward other Noachide groups). Online: http://www.noahide.com/prayer.htm.

33. Michael Dallen, "Prayer, How Should Noahides Pray?" Online: http://rainbowcovenant.org/pages/noahideworship.htm. The sense of inaccessibility to Jewish prayer is true for many people, including Jews.

34. Http://www.okbns.org/Free.html ("Daily Prayers," iii). I agree with Katz that Gentiles should not say anything in prayer that is a lie, such as "who has commanded us" about something they have not been commanded to do. In contrast to Katz, I think that Gentile believers can say that God took "us" out of Egypt, based on 1 Cor 10:1, as presented above.

35. R. Kendall Soulen, *The God of Israel and Christian Theology*, 111.

36. Luke T. Johnson, *The Writings of the New Testament* (Philadelphia: Fortress, 1986), 378–79.

In a larger picture, the benefits of mutual blessing by diverse people require that those people remain distinct in some ways. God gives different gifts to different people for the upbuilding of the body of Messiah (1 Cor 12). The social face of justification—God's activity to make things right through Yeshua—is the *ekklesia* composed of Jews and Gentiles.[37] It is what Martin Luther King, Jr., meant by "the Beloved Community."

Practical Aspects of Gentiles Praying in the Synagogue

In this last section, I will address prayers in the regular Sabbath services that might be problematic for Gentile Yeshua-believers.

1. Blessing before study of the Torah

The traditional liturgy speaks (a) of being commanded (i.e. "who has sanctified us with his commandments and commanded us to engross ourselves in the words of Torah"); (b) of Israel as "we," "us," and "our offspring." The blessing when called to the Torah scroll includes those words "who chose us from all peoples" and "who gave us the Torah."

A Noachide blessing before reading the Torah states that God gave the Torah "to be a light to the Gentiles." The blessing lacks mention of being commanded, and calls Israel "them." After reading the Torah, the Noachide blesses God for giving Israel to teach "us" the Torah.[38] These blessings seem acceptable for Gentiles in a Messianic synagogue as well. Some Yeshua-believers prefer them because the distinction between Jew and Gentile is clear.

If a Gentile believer wished to use something closer to, or even identical to the traditional Jewish blessings for Torah study, it is essential to have a proper and special intention (*kavvanah*). The individual's intention should be to affirm a unity with Israel through Yeshua as a Gentile, and that all the things spoken are true concerning Israel. In my view, Torah study is an activity that a Gentile believer in Yeshua may speak of being commanded to do. There is even a communal aspect to the bless-

37. The Roeh Yisrael Messianic Jewish congregation in Jerusalem has this goal. It strives to imitate the community of Yeshua's first-century disciples, Jews who were diligent in their observance of the Torah, who lived as an integral part of the Jewish community, and who believed in Yeshua as Messiah. The pattern in that community is one of cultural pluralism—Jews who remain Jews and Gentiles who remain Gentiles, all worshiping the Lord together.

38. See Chavurath B'Nei Noach, online: http://webpages.charter.net/chavurathbneinoach/FAQs. html.

ing. For a Jew who has no offspring, the traditional blessing can be said because the offspring of other Jews are "our offspring." This provides additional support for the Gentile believer in Yeshua to include himself or herself in the "we" of Israel.

2. *The* Shema *(Deut 6:4–9; Deut 11:13–21; Num 15:37–41)*

The *Shema* is an intellectual commitment to the unity, grandeur, and absolute authority of God. While for prayer, God is Thou (You), in the *Shema*, God is addressed in the third person (He).[39]

Yehoshua ben Korhah said, "Why is 'Hear O Israel' ('*Shema*,' Deut 6:4–9) recited before 'If, then, you obey the commandments' (Deut 11:13–21) in the daily prayers? To indicate that one must first accept the kingdom of heaven, and only afterwards the yoke of the commandments" (*m. Ber.* 2:2). According to Yoel Schwartz, it is worthwhile for a Noachide to regularly repeat basic concepts of belief such as "*Shema Yisrael*."[40]

Yeshua taught about the kingdom of heaven in the Sermon on the Mount and in parables and sayings, "Your kingdom come, your will be done on earth as it is in heaven" (Matt 6:10). Yeshua said that to love the Lord your God with all your heart, soul, mind and strength (Deut 6:5) is the greatest commandment (Mark 12:29–30). It is highly appropriate for a Gentile believer to regularly recite the *Shema*, which with the proper kavvanah is accepting the yoke of heaven.[41]

However, it is possible that a Gentile believer would do well to recite only the first three sentences of the *Shema*,[42] rather than the later paragraphs dealing with commandments, or even the first full paragraph where it speaks of *tefillin* and *mezuzah*. Having said this, I find it unpleasant to think of changing my habit of saying the entire *Shema*. The emotions evoked by the intense concentration on God's unity,

---

39. Joseph B. Soloveitchik, *Worship of the Heart: Essays on Jewish Prayer* (ed. Shalom Carmy; New York: Toras HaRav Foundation/KTAV, 2003), 96.

40. Yoel Schwartz, "The Noahide Commandments," Chapter 1, http://www.geocities.com/Rachav/Chapter1_Rav_Schwartz.htm?20067.

41. In "Prayer in Yeshua, Prayer in Israel: The Shema in Messianic Perspective" (2008 Hashivenu Forum), Mark Kinzer proposes a kavvanah in which Yeshua infuses the traditional liturgy.

42. At the Narkis Street Christian congregation in Jerusalem, the first paragraph of the *Shema* and the commandment to love one's neighbor as oneself (Lev 19:8) are recited together in Hebrew, following the example of Yeshua (Mark 12:29–31; Luke 10:27). In the B'nai Noach siddur, the *Shema* consists of Deut 6:4 (and response), Gen 2:16, Gen 9:4, and Deut 6:6–7.

grandeur, and authority are not in harmony with an abbreviation that resembles turning away while God is speaking.

Of particular relevance for a Gentile believer is Paul's connection of God's unity to the gospel, "God who is one will justify the circumcised out of faithfulness and the uncircumcised through the same faithfulness" (Rom 3:30).[43]

Eberhard Bethge was the closest disciple of Dietrich Bonhoeffer and his biographer. Bethge saw the church under the Third Reich compromise its identity by granting highest allegiance to the Fuhrer. Bethge later formulated a Christian *Shema* in response to the First Commandment, "I confess my allegiance to the Christ, who brings us God and life, who turns our thoughts against false gods and toward those who are their victims."[44]

3. Prayer recalling martyrs

A prayer asks God, *Av-ha-Rachamim* (the Compassionate Father), to recall with compassion "the devout, the upright, the perfect ones, the holy congregations who gave their lives for the sanctification of the Name." Some *siddurim* contain a note here about the Jewish communities along the Rhine that were destroyed by Christians at the time of the Crusades.[45]

While I think it is appropriate for a Gentile believer to recite the prayer, I have three preferences with regard to it. First, I ask God to remember the dead; I don't pray on behalf of the dead. Second, even though many Christian martyrs died in early centuries for refusing to worship the Roman Emperor, and Anabaptist Christian martyrs died during the Reformation at the hands of Protestants and Catholics, and there are Christian martyrs also in our times, I suggest that Gentile believers concentrate upon Jewish martyrs during the first part of the prayer. Christian martyrs may be recalled while reciting the words "with the other righteous of the world." Third, my practice is to end the prayer with "righteous of the world," rather than reading the remainder of the prayer, which asks for God's vengeance for the spilled blood of his servants. In part, that is because of my notions of what is appropriate for Shabbat.

---

43. The faithfulness ("keeping faith") of God through the faith/faithfulness of Yeshua. For an introduction to the translation issues, see Harink, *Paul Among the Postliberals*, 26–30.

44. Eberhard Bethge, "Christology and the First Commandment," *Holocaust and Genocide Studies* 4:3 (1989): 261–72.

45. See the ArtScroll siddur, Nusach Ashkenaz. The prayer is not part of the Sephardic liturgy.

4. Interpreting the Amidah using rabbinic categories of thought

Believers in Yeshua who pray from the *siddur* may be inclined to interpret the traditional Jewish liturgy in Christian categories of thought. I shall not challenge this preference other than to relate that I have benefited from rabbinic guidance into the spirit of Jewish prayer.

The central prayer in the Jewish liturgy is the *Amidah* (literally, "standing [before God]"). On weekdays the *Amidah* consists of three benedictions of praise, thirteen containing petitions, and three statements of thanksgiving. On the Sabbath and festivals, the middle section of thirteen is replaced by a benediction related to the day.

According to Joseph Soloveitchik, the form of the *Amidah* presupposes that the emotions it articulates—praise, distress, and gratitude—are legitimate and that ordinary human beings are capable of experiencing them, "Education to prayer teaches not only how to verbalize these emotions, but also how to cultivate them."[46] Soloveitchik develops his analysis out of biblical and rabbinic sources and in conversation with Western philosophy.

Humans have intellectual, ethical, and aesthetic facets to their being. The intellectual and ethical are oriented toward what is good, true and purposeful, and hence seek expression through permanence and uniformity in prayer. The aesthetic sense is oriented toward beauty, and hence seeks expression through change and novelty. When the aesthetic sense is not connected to purpose, through the intellectual and ethical senses, it results in boredom.

According to Maimonides and Nahmanides, the original sin resulted from the aesthetic sense (tangible, mutable perception) dominating the intellectual and ethical senses (which are abstract and metaphysical). Maimonides considered the knowledge of good and evil to refer not to moral qualities but to aesthetic ones, as shown by the characterization of the tree in the garden as good for success, rather than knowledge, and a delight to the eyes (Gen 3:6). Correspondingly, Adam and Eve perceived after eating from the tree that they were naked, which reflects a social, aesthetic sense (embarrassment), not a moral, self-accusing one (shame).[47]

The aesthetic is redeemed by being brought into relation with something beyond it, i.e. the exaltation of God (Isa 6:1-3). In fact, only through the aesthetic sense does a person apprehend and not merely comprehend God's presence, which

---

46. Soloveitchik, *Worship of the Heart: Essays on Jewish Prayer*, xii.

47. Ibid., 45–49.

is awesome, both beautiful and exalted.[48] Jewish prayer joins the aesthetic, intellectual, and ethical.

Judaism maintains that humanity encounters God in both nature and the message of history, but the absence of God is also encountered in both realms. Judaism recognizes these moments of absence as part of a larger story culminating in redemption. Redemption is not simply an external event that benefits the individual or the group. "It is predicated on the formation of community with God."[49] Through prayer, which is possible only because God has told us to pray, a community comes into being. This community is an antidote to the loneliness that results from lack of roots and a sense of estrangement.

In the first blessing of the *Amidah*, the Lord is called the God of our fathers, full of mercy. Like a father, God hears our cries with love and favor. The second blessing emphasizes God's power in contrast to human weakness, but God shows his power by mercifully raising the dead. The blessing teaches how to approach God from an ethical standpoint. The third blessing teaches God's absolute separation (holiness), yet that God can be approached.

5. Prayers that appear to express wrong approaches to God

In the weekday morning and Sabbath afternoon service after *Uva L'tsion Goel* (a Redeemer shall come to Zion) is a prayer which in English reads as follows:

> Blessed is our God, who created us for His glory, separated us from those who stray, gave us the Torah of truth and implanted eternal life within us. May He open our heart through His Torah and imbue our heart with love and awe of Him that we may do His will and serve him wholeheartedly, so that we do not struggle in vain nor produce for futility.
>
> May it be Your will, Lord our God and the God of our fathers, that we observe Your decrees in This World, and merit (or *be worthy*) that we live and see and inherit goodness and blessing in this world (others read, *the years of the Messianic times*) and for the life of the World to Come. Grant that I may sing Your praise and not be silent, Lord my God, I will praise you forever.

The first blessing may be problematic for Yeshua-believers because, by thanking God for separating one from those who err, it vaguely resembles the prayer of the

---

48. Ibid., 58–62.

49. Ibid., xxii.

Pharisee who thanked God for not being like the tax colletor (Luke 18:14). The second section asks that one be accounted by God to have merit, which may appear to promote self-righteousness. By contrast, Yeshua seems to have taught that, when you have done all that is commanded, you should say, "We are unworthy (or *unprofitable*) servants" (Luke 17:10).

Upon closer examination, neither objection is valid. These paragraphs ask of God for the right actions and the right heart, and do not claim self-righteousness. They follow the tone established by earlier prayers that request, "Do not bring us into the power of error" and "Not in the merit of our righteousness do we cast our supplications before You, but in the merit of Your abundant mercy." Wyschogrod comments on the first request, "When Paul says that humans are not justified by works of the Law, this is exactly what he means."[50]

Yeshua did not separate from tax collectors, nor did he separate from Pharisees. However, Yeshua did gather a group about him whose composition and way of life were in contrast to the larger culture. Yoder has observed that only such a contrast group can critique and provide a viable alternative to the dominant culture.[51] In this sense, of the body of Messiah and the people of Israel as contrast communities, should the prayer "who has separated us from those who stray" be understood.

The New Testament teaches in many places that persons will be judged by their deeds.[52] Thankfully, the prayer that it may be God's will that we observe commandments and merit reward does not violate the attitude of humility taught by Yeshua.

Some prayers for healing of the sick ask that God answer the request *b'zchar zeh* ("in the merit of this"), referring either to the merit of the act of praying, or of giving charity. While I agree that it is good to pray for others and to give to charity, I suggest that the prayers make sense and should be recited without *b'zchar zeh*. Conceivably, one could also have in mind a merit other than something performed by the ones praying.

In one Messianic congregation, worshipers omit the *Amidah* paragraph which states that God did not give the Sabbath, or its rest, to the nations of the earth. These words are thought by them not to match the New Testament teachings that both Jews and non-Jews are equally loved and that Shabbat is for everyone who chooses

---

50. Wyschogrod, "Paul, Jews, and Gentiles," in *Abraham's Promise*, 199.

51. John H.Yoder, "How H. Richard Niebuhr Reasoned: A Critique of *Christ and Culture*," in *Authentic Transformation: A New Vision of Christ and Culture*.

52. See Mark S. Kinzer, "Final Destinies: Qualifications for Receiving an Eschatological Inheritance" *Kesher* 22 (Spring/Summer 2008): 87–119.

to enjoy its blessing.[53] I suppose this omission may be an improvement, but it is not my practice.

6. Statements that appear to conflict with Christian claims about Yeshua

A stanza, "There never arose in Israel another like Moses" (Deut 34:10), from *Yigdal*, seems to imply that no prophet greater than Moses has appeared. One possible approach to this prayer focuses on the meaning of "in Israel." Yeshua, although a faithful son of Israel, has not attained a position within Israel comparable to Moses. It is only outside Israel—in the church (or heaven)—that Yeshua is elevated above Moses. A second approach is to recognize that *Yigdal* is what Krister Stendahl calls "caressing, love talk," the language of confession and worship.[54] As love talk, recitation of *Yigdal* would be permitted to those for whom Maimonides' Thirteen Articles of Faith (which *Yigdal* renders poetically) could not be recited.

According to David Stern and Elazar Brandt, some Messianic congregations in Israel omit from the prayer *Adon Olam* the statement "He is one, there is no second," because the prayer's author meant to reject Yeshua. Stern and Brandt rightly counter that (trinitarian) belief in Yeshua is not polytheism, but is in keeping with Isaiah 45 (cf. Phil 2:10–11), from which the stanza is drawn. "Those omitting the stanza may implicitly be admitting the polytheism they are falsely accused of."[55]

Prayers for the Temple to be rebuilt might seem to contravene the efficacy of Yeshua's sacrifice for sin.[56] However, one may pray for a physical Temple by adopting one rabbinic opinion that no expiatory sacrifices will be offered in the future.

Alternatively, God's house may be envisioned as God's people, as in Numbers 12:7 and Hebrews 3:5–6. The rebuilding of God's house may allude to the reconciliation of Jews and Gentiles (Isa 56:7–8), but without loss of distinction between parties. Abraham Isaac Kook said in another context that the Temple was destroyed

---

53. I thank Beth Broadway of Roeh Israel/Netivyah Bible Instruction Ministry for this information.

54. Krister Stendahl, "Christ's Lordship and Religious Pluralism," in *Meanings: The Bible as Document and as Guide* (Philadelphia: Fortress, 1984), 233–244.

55. David H. Stern and Elazar Brandt, "The Use of Liturgy in Messianic Jewish Worship," *Mishkan* 25 (1996).

56. Derek Leman ("Understanding the Sacrifices of Israel, Past and Future" [n.p.]) points out, however, that in Acts 21:26, Paul presented a sin offering. Leman argues that this was not contrary to the atoning death of Yeshua..

because of hatred for no reason, and it will only be rebuilt as a result of love for no reason.

7. Prayers that can be said in Hebrew but not in the usual English translation

The Hebrew word "*goy*" can take on either the meaning "Gentile" or "nation." Exodus 32:10–14 recounts that God "offered" to destroy Israel and make of Moses a great nation, but Moses demurred, and God relented. There is a tradition that Moses recited the blessing "who has not made me a *goy*" (found in the siddur) right after this. Moses thanked God that God did not make him a "*goy*" (nation), replacing the nation of Israel. This interpretation is especially appropriate for a Christian because it is a disavowal of displacement theology. The usual translation, which thanks God for not having created one a Gentile, of course cannot be said by a Gentile.

In some *siddurim*, three prayers in the negative ("who has not made me") are replaced by one thanking God for having conferred upon the person praying the obligations of a Jew. For a Gentile believer, a substitute prayer might thank God for having laid upon the worshiper the yoke of the kingdom of heaven and the yoke of Yeshua. Alternately, one could thank God "who has created me according to your will,"[57] or "who has allowed me freedom to serve you."[58]

The opening paragraph of the *Amidah* concludes, "He will bring a redeemer. . . ." Some Messianic Jews feel this is unacceptable, since God has already sent a redeemer in Yeshua. I don't find the text problematic. However, for those who disagree, a solution would be changing the English text to "he brings," which is consistent with the Hebrew.[59]

8. Prayers that may not be said in the usual form, although the connected activity is acceptable

Writing for Noachides, Yoel Schwartz affirms that a Gentile should not observe the Sabbath in the manner that a Jew does, nor give a Jew an occasion to break the Sabbath.

57. An expression from the traditional siddur. R. Kendall Soulen (*The God of Israel and Christian Theology*, 88) finds a positive identity in the term *Gentile*, "The term *Gentile* implies actual participation in covenant history because it conceives of (non-Jewish) humanity within the horizon of Israel's particular election."

58. *Service of the Heart, Daily Prayers*, 3. Online: http://www.okbns.org/Free.html.

59. Stern and Brandt, "The Use of Liturgy in Messianic Jewish Worship."

There are those who say that every *Ger Toshav* (a non-Jew living in *Eretz Yisrael* in the time of the Jewish Temple, who has formally accepted the obligation to observe the Noahide laws in front of a Jewish court) has to uphold and keep the Sabbath (Rashi, *Kritot* 9, *Yevamot* 40). There is room to suggest that the Noahides, even nowadays, by accepting to fulfill the seven commandments, are in the same category as a *Ger Toshav* and should, according to Rashi, be required or at least allowed to keep the Sabbath.

So I (Rav Schwartz) would like to suggest that this is the way that the Noahides could celebrate the Seventh Day, a day of refraining from his vocation. On the eve of the Sabbath (Friday night), they might have a festive family dinner with special food and light candles after sundown in honor of the Seventh Day, which was given to Adam and Noah (and to make the Noachide celebration of the Shabbat distinct from the Jewish Shabbat observance). During the meal they may sing songs to strengthen their belief, including songs about creation. They may read from the Torah. They should not call this day the Sabbath, but the Seventh Day as it is written in Genesis.

On the Seventh Day itself, if they can arrange it without difficulty, they should refrain from going to work. If possible, they should go out to the fields or a park so as to feel close to the Creator of the world. If the congregation holds a prayer session, they may recite the Psalms connected to the Sabbath and to the creation (like Psalm 104, "the Blessing of the Soul"). Also they should study portions of the Torah connected to commandments of the children of Noah. They can study from the weekly portion of the Torah being read that Sabbath in the synagogues those subjects which concern all mankind and skipping those topics that concern specifically the Jews.

At the end of the Sabbath (*Motzai Shabbat*), the end of the Seventh Day and the beginning of the new week, they can recite the prayer for the new week (*Havdalah*) after having lighted a candle. . . . [60]

Schwartz is a senior lecturer at Yeshivat Dvar Yerushalaim, the author of two books on Bnei Noach, and one who has given an approbation for the Bnei Noach siddur. If he allows some Jewish rituals for Gentiles, they should almost certainly be allowed within Messianic Judaism. I would go further than Schwartz because I believe that Yeshua links the Gentile *ekklesia* to Israel. I have no objection to a Gentile believer,

60. Yoel Schwartz, "The Noahide Commandments," Chapter 1. Online: http://www.geocities.com/Rachav/Chapter1_Rav_Schwartz.htm?20067.

with correct *kavvanah*, saying "Shabbat" instead of "Seventh Day," reading any portion of Scripture, and doing some other Jewish practices. With Schwartz, I would
suggest making some changes to Jewish practices for Gentiles, such as not saying
"who has commanded us to light the Sabbath candles," or "who has commanded us
regarding the washing of hands," for the sake of distinguishing Jew from Gentile.[61]

9. Prayers that may not be said by a Gentile, nor may the connected activity be performed

Schwartz writes:

> Noahides may perform commandments that were given specifically to the
> Jews in the hope that they will be rewarded for them, provided that they
> don't consider these actions obligatory. It is also important to note that
> according to some opinions there are some commandments that Noahides
> should not fulfill because they are connected with holiness and given spe-
> cifically to Israel. These are the commandments of *Tefillin* and *mezuzah*.[62]

There is no agreement in Messianic Judaism as to activities that a Gentile may not
perform. A visible example of variation is the wearing of the *tallit* (prayer shawl) by
a Gentile, which in some congregations is routine, or is expected only for special
honors such as carrying a Torah scroll, or is never an option. Messianic congregations should at least agree to the principle of making a distinction between Jews
and non-Jews, and that for this purpose Gentiles should not engage in some ritual
activities.

Yochanan ben Zakkai said that a corpse would not defile, nor would water pu-
rify, were it not a decree of God (*Pesiq. Rab. Kah.* 4:7; *Num. Rab.* 19:8). The apostle
Paul agreed with the underlying position that some biblical commandments transcend reason. Therefore, if they are commanded only to Jews, they are for Jews but

---

61. Similarly, H. Bruce Stokes writes, "In our home, we celebrate the Sabbath in a manner similar,
but not identical, to the traditions of Judaism. All of the Torah's commands and elements of Judaism are
present. But the form is distinct. Our Jewish neighbors who know of our observance sometimes express
a desire to have what is rightfully theirs. They see an authenticity in what we do that reminds them of
childhood Sabbaths at home. We are often asked why we observe the Sabbath. We respond with the
text from Isaiah 56:6–8 which tells of the Gentiles who keep the Sabbath. Jewish and Gentile believers
must work together to protect our separate identities while becoming one new man in the Body of the
Messiah" ("Gentiles in the Messianic Movement," online: http://www.imja.com/Stokes.html).

62. Yoel Schwartz, "The Noahide Commandments," Chapter 1. Online: http://www.geocities.com/
Rachav/Chapter1_Rav_Schwartz.htm?20067.

not for Gentiles. As Paul diplomatically put it, "nothing is unclean in itself; but it is unclean for anyone who thinks it unclean" (Rom 14:14).[63]

For any Jewish activity that a Gentile declines to participate in exactly as a Jew does,[64] I can see three options: (1) to copy the practice closely so that a casual observer would not notice, while still making a distinction; (2) substituting another ritual whose distinctivness is evident to a casual observer;[65] (3) for the Gentile to abstain from the Jewish activity. The second option of noticeable substitution perhaps in a Messianic synagogue interferes with the institutional goal of being a recognizable Jewish worship space. The problem might be ameliorated by strengthening the Jewish behavior of Jewish congregants, or by using a tradition that is not associated with triumphalism or persecution of Jews, or by placing the activity before or after the Jewish worship service, rather than within it. The second and third options may cause Gentile worshipers to feel disconnected from Jewish worshipers. If Gentile believers are to feel integrated into a Jewish congregation, they may need to compensate for perceived liturgical exclusion by fuller participation in other aspects of congregational life

10. Praying like a Jew, when one has good reasons not to

At home and when alone, a Gentile can emulate prayers and rituals found in the Messianic or other synagogue.[66] Joshua Massey observes:

---

63. Kinzer, *Postmissionary Messianic Judaism*, 55–57.

64. Barney Kasdan proposes to define and strengthen Jewish/Gentile distinctives in the Messianic synagogue through education, coupled with processes for affiliation and confirmation. Kay Silberling would resolve tensions through introducing liturgical practices that more fully enfranchise non-Jews *qua* non-Jews. Douglas Harink encourages the explicit and intentional affirmation and celebration of the Gentile-ness of Gentiles. See *Kesher* 19 (Summer 2005): 41, 73, 85. The Tikkun Ministries International staff writers offer suggestions for celebrating the Feast of First Fruits in a Gentile way without ever using Jewish liturgy or Hebrew language ("Which Law Do We Keep?" Online: www .tikkunministries.org/articles/jack-whichlaw.htm). For a happy addition to the havdalah prayer, see *Service of the Heart*, "Remembering the Seventh Day," 33, online: http://www.okbns.org/Free.html. After a traditional listing of distinctions between days, between light and dark, and Israel and the nations, the following is added, "and between Jews and Gentiles, who together are partners in one holy objective, to make your name One throughout the world."

65. Not every activity that seems distinctive to Judaism is absent from Christianity. There exist Christian traditions of saying the Grace After Meals, and 1 Timothy 4:4–5 gives a Christian precedent for blessing God in all activities of daily life.

66. Cornelius kept the Jewish time for prayer (Acts 10:3). See Joshua Massey, "Living Like Jesus, a Torah Observant Jew: Delighting in God's Law for Incarnational Witness to Muslims,"

> As Jesus said, "*A disciple . . . when he is fully taught will be like his teacher*" (Luke 6:40). . . . If one practices these forms [e.g. prays Jewish prayers] with an inner appreciation of their sacred significance before God—if they have become deeply *personal*—then there can be no charge of masquerade, façade, or incongruity within or without.[67]

When praying in "Jewish space," a Gentile believer balances the imperatives of identification and non-identification with the Jewish people, along with other values. When not in "Jewish space," the Gentile believer continues to balance these values, but the relative weights of each change with the situation. Ideally, one should not be lax about identification with the Jewish people, but strict about expressing and strengthening one's unique identity, which is essential for the mutual blessing of Israel and the nations.

Throughout their lives, diverse values (such as amity with non-Jewish relatives) may influence Gentiles to avoid certain Jewish activities. Sometimes this is the priority, all the more so since Gentiles are not Jews. They will have different obligations than Jews, not necessarily lesser ones.[68] I internalize the value of difference and therefore refrain from some Jewish practices even though they are personally gratifying, for the sake of furthering the vision of mutual blessing.

---

67 *International Journal of Frontier Missions* 21:2 (2004). Online: http://www.ijfm.org/PDFs_IJFM/21_2_PDFs/Massey.pdf. Massey explores the dilemma of the Christian missionary among Muslims who adopts Muslim behaviors for the sake of contextual witness, but later comes to feel inauthentic when acting differently in private. Massey offers the alternative of incarnational living. I do not pray like a Jew, and among Jews, in order to convert Jews. Rather, I endorse the following approach to evangelism, when evangelism is appropriate: "As we share our story in the context of authentic relationships, we are liberated from a savior syndrome. We are freed to enter into new relationships with people everywhere supported by the conviction that we have come to learn, to be enriched, indeed to be completed. In that space of engagement, we must still fully share our own narrative. For Anabaptists that narrative includes the Bible, centered on Jesus, the gift of God for the salvation of the world and the One in whom all things hold together (Eph. 1:17–23). The story also includes the centuries of commitment to reconciliation and peacemaking. If such sharing attracts others to incorporate this story as part of their narrative, then we must celebrate this as the work of God who effects conversion by the Holy Spirit. As Anabaptists, it would be disingenuous and antithetical to the core of our identity to deny this possibility. Whether through the vicissitudes of history or intentional theological choice, Anabaptists have embraced a pilgrim identity. For pilgrim people, borders and building bridges are part of the fabric of life." See Stanley Green's Foreword in *Borders and Bridges: Mennonite Witness in a Religiously Diverse World*. Online: http://www.pandorapressus.com/bab/babfore.htm.

68. All who believe in Yeshua are called to discipleship. I have found John Howard Yoder to be helpful in explicating the various forms of possible obedience. The crucial roles and inclusion of outsiders in the Bible is the theme of Frank Anthony Spina's *The Faith of the Outsider*.

> When they work well, religious congregations function as communities
> of obligation, not as spaces for individual gratification. Communities of
> obligation pose expectations to which individuals voluntarily submit, and
> which over time become such a part of individuals' identities that they are,
> in a sense, binding.[69]

If Gentile believers in Yeshua are clear about their position before God, their relationship to Judaism, the Jewish people, and all their communities of obligation, they
will weigh their choices well, making decisions that please and glorify God.

Conclusion

Gentile believers are joined to Israel through Yeshua. The Jewish people rightly express their covenantal relationship to God in part through behavior that distinguishes
them from Gentiles. However, the Tanakh and New Testament envision the mutual
blessing, and prayer together, of Jews and Gentiles who remain different. Therefore,
Gentile believers need to hold in balance the contrasting values of unity and separation with regard to Jews, both Yeshua-believers and non-Yeshua-believers.

How a Gentile might pray as a Jew can be stated in general, but not in detail,
as individual preferences matter, and rightly so. Gentile believers can address God
with great freedom, and love him with their whole hearts, within the framework of
identification with, yet distinction from, the people of Israel.

JON C. OLSON (DPM, DrPH) lives in the Hartford, Connecticut area with his
wife, Susan. He participates in a Mennonite fellowship and religiously identifies as
Mennonite, while regularly praying with three congregations: Orthodox Jewish,
Messianic Jewish, and Christian. He is an epidemiologist at a state health department, and teaches in a graduate public health program. Professional and contact
information for him are online at http://www.umass.edu/sphhs/mph_online/faculty
.html.

69. Robert Wuthnow, *American Mythos: Why Our Best Efforts to be a Better Nation Fall Short*
(Princeton: Princeton University Press, 2006), 215.

Complexity in Early Jewish Messianism

JOSHUA BRUMBACH

"For in Him all the fullness of Deity dwells in bodily form, and in
Him you have been made complete, and he is the head over all rule
and authority"

Col 2:9–10

"Yeshua said to her, 'I Am the Resurrection and the Life! Whoever
puts [their] trust in me will live, even if [they] die; and everyone living and trusting in me will never die. Do you believe this?' She said
to him, 'Yes, Lord, I believe that you are the Messiah, the Son of God,
the one coming into the world'"

John 11:25–27

There is a popular assumption in Jewish circles that Judaism has never believed in
a divine Messiah. Some argue that Yeshua himself never claimed to be the Messiah
and that his earliest followers would never have considered him to be God. Professor
Israel Knohl of Hebrew University in Jerusalem comments:

> Scholars of this viewpoint maintain that Jesus did not regard himself as the
> Messiah at all and that his disciples proclaimed him the Messiah after his
> death. Jesus, they claim, could not have foreseen his rejection, death, and
> resurrection, as 'the idea of a suffering, dying, and rising Messiah or son of
> Man was unknown to Judaism.'[1]

But can this view be supported? To understand the ideology of these earliest
disciples, it is incumbent to understand the first-century Jewish world as well as
the broader influence of ideas that existed within Ancient Near Eastern thought.
Dietmar Neufeld, of the University of British Columbia, confirms that, "a heavenly,

---

1. Israel Knohl, *The Messiah Before Jesus* (Berkeley: University of California Press, 2000), 2. The
word "Messiah," or משיח (*mashiach*) in Hebrew, simply means "Anointed One."

transcendent Messiah was not a unique invention of the Christian community but the outgrowth of reflection that had its roots in Judaism."[2] The roots of the early Yeshua followers are in the pluralistic Judaisms of the period. In order to delve into the views of the early "believing" community regarding the person of Yeshua, it is vital to understand the differences between the Jewish world then, and Judaism as it would later become.

The concept of the Messiah in Jewish thought was far more complex before the destruction of the Second Temple (70 CE) than after. Neufeld contends, "contrary to traditional assumptions of an ubiquitous and consistent messianism in early Judaism, numerous recent studies have pointed out that messianism was a fluid and diverse phenomenon."[3] Over time, the established Jewish leadership refrained from defining the messiah in exalted terms, since radical messianism was explained to be a cause for the destruction of the Temple and Israel's dispersion. According to Kay Smith, of Azusa Pacific University, "from approximately the 3rd century BCE, to the 2nd century CE, the Jewish world was very pluralistic. During the Second Temple period, Jews interpreted and interacted with their scriptures differently than today."[4]

During this period, we see varying strains within the Jewish world—radical apocalypticism, messianism, monasticism, etc. Mark Nanos, in his book *The Mystery of Romans*, writes, "Judaism tolerated many different views . . . This pluralism extended throughout Judaism and blended even the distinctions between Palestinian and Diaspora beliefs and practices so that it is not possible to speak of a monolithic or normative Judaism."[5] This pluralism influenced the way each group interacted with, and interpreted, the world around them. There was no one way to be a Jew, or to interpret a particular text. Concerning this period, scholars cannot say with any kind of certainty, "This is what Jews believed or practiced." There was disagreement over everything—calendar, lineage of the priesthood, sacrifices, canon, even the primary locus of ritual observance.[6] This complexity extended to Jewish conceptions

2. Dietmar Neufeld. "And When That One Comes: Aspects of Johannine Messianism." *Eschatology, Messianism, and the Dead Sea Scrolls.* Ed. Graig A. Evans and Peter W. Flint. (Grand Rapids: Eerdmans Publishing, 1997), 140.

3. Ibid. Neufeld, 120.

4. Kay Silberling Smith, *The Messiah of Israel* (Unpublished Lecture Notes—Beth Emunah Messianic Synagogue, Agoura Hills, CA, 1997).

5. Mark D. Nanos, *The Mystery of Romans* (Minneapolis: Fortress Press, 1996), 42.

6. This is reflected in Qumran, and to a lesser extent in the earliest community of Yeshua followers. See Geza Vermes, *The Complete Dead Sea Scrolls in English* (New York: Penguin Books, 1997), 24, 78–79, etc.

of the Messiah and other divine agents. William Horbury asserts that "some biblical redeemer-figures which are often reckoned as angelic rather than messianic in modern study were interpreted messianically in antiquity."[7] Smith further notes:

> It was extremely common (may I say extremely 'Jewish') during this period to write about an exalted agent of God with characteristics of the divine and still be a monotheist . . . Jews were comfortable with the notion of a single, exalted figure, who had all the characteristics of God and did all the things that God does, who was exalted above all others, present with God at creation, but . . . *and this is the most important element* . . . they in no sense thought this was betraying the classical confession, Hear O Israel, the Lord is our God, the Lord is One.[8]

Thus, belief in divine agents was not viewed as a violation of the belief in "only One God." The early Jewish followers did not see themselves as practicing idolatry, or worshiping a foreign god by proclaiming Yeshua's divinity. According to Larry Hurtado of the University of Edinburgh, "all evidence indicates . . . that those Jewish [believers] who made such a step remained convinced that they were truly serving the God of the Old Testament."[9] He adds:

> The cultic veneration of Jesus as a divine figure apparently began among Jewish [believers], whose religious background placed great emphasis upon the uniqueness of God. It is evident that their devotion had its own distinct shape, a kind of binitarian reverence which included both God and the exalted Jesus . . . apparently they regarded this redefinition not only as legitimate, but, indeed, as something demanded of them.[10]

The view that the Messiah would be more than human goes back as far as Isaiah and Jeremiah. These authors believed in something approximating a divine Messiah:

> The idea that the Messiah or the king at the end of days is a figure with divine attributes is already found in the Bible. The prophet Isaiah used the expression 'mighty God' in this connection (9:5), and Jeremiah said that the king at the end of days would be called 'the Lord our righteousness' (23:6).[11]

7. William Horbury, *Messianism Among Jews and Christians* (London: T&T Clark, 2003), 57.

8. Ibid. Silberling Smith.

9. Larry W. Hurtado, *One God, One Lord: Early Christian Devotion and Ancient Jewish Monotheism* (Philadelphia: Fortress Press, 1998), 14.

10. Ibid., 11.

11. Ibid. Knohl, 84.

Knohl goes on to note that this motif is "connected with the 'suffering servant' in Isaiah 53 . . . The figure described . . . combines characteristics of God, [and] the king-Messiah."[12]

The Dead Sea Scrolls reflect this development in messianic thought. Texts describe an exalted figure who would suffer and die, only to be resurrected.[13] This understanding has been brought to the forefront of scholarly debate with the recently published inscription known as "Gabriel's Revelation."[14] This apocalyptic inscription, written on stone, dates to the late first century BCE, or the early first century CE.[15] Although some of the text is difficult to read, Knohl contends that it refers to a suffering Messiah who is to be resurrected within three days.[16] This idea seems quite different from the commonly held assumptions about a victorious Messiah Son of David. According to Knohl, "The new inscription, 'Gabriel's Revelation,' suggests that this different kind of Messiah was evolving at the turn of the era—different from the Messiah son of David. Instead of a militant Messiah, it envisions a Messiah who suffered, died, and rose."[17]

Other scholars concurs with this assessment. Hershel Shanks of the Biblical Archaeology Society writes:

> By Jesus' time . . . the concept of the *mashiach* had developed beyond that of an earthly messiah who would restore the glory of the kingdom of David. It also came to mean a divinely sent figure who would return as God's agent and usher in the world to come. The Dead Sea Scrolls reflect this development . . . thus . . . the messiah was already freighted with eschatological content.[18]

The eschatological conception of the Son of God was also extant in Second Temple Judaism. As Shanks puts it, "that divine sonship is present in the Dead Sea Scrolls before Jesus is declared the Son of God should not be surprising."[19]

---

12. Ibid., 84.

13. Ibid., 37–50.

14. Israel Knohl, "The Messiah Son of Joseph." *Biblical Archaeology Review,* September/October 2008.

15. Ibid, 58.

16. Ibid, 60–61.

17. Ibid, 62.

18. Hershel Shanks, *The Mystery and Meaning of the Dead Sea Scrolls* (New York: Random House, 1998), 68–69.

19. Ibid., 69.

The early Yeshua followers were convinced that Yeshua was a divine Messiah, and their understanding was based on Jewish understandings. Paul wrote in the early years after Yeshua: "It is through his Son that we have redemption, that is, our sins have been forgiven. *He is the visible image of the invisible God.* He is supreme over all creation, because in connection with him were created all things—in heaven and on earth, visible and invisible . . . He existed before all things, and he holds everything together—" (Col 1:14–17).

Did Yeshua believe that he was the Messiah? The Gospels do not record Yeshua using the words "I am the Messiah." Nevertheless, evidence from the Apostolic Writings suggests that Yeshua did indeed believe himself to be an exalted figure, not only a wonder-working teacher and deliverer, but God incarnate.

As an example, in the Gospel of John, Yeshua states: "Most assuredly, I say to you, before Abraham was, I AM" (John 8:58). This declaration points directly to the God of Israel in the Hebrew Bible (Exodus 3:14) and connotes eternal attributes.

During Chanukah in Jerusalem, Yeshua was approached by a number of worshipers in the Temple, and was asked directly, "How much longer are you going to keep us in suspense? If you are the Messiah, tell us publicly!" (John 10:24). In response to their inquiry, Yeshua said, "I and the Father are one" (John 10:30). Yeshua indeed saw himself to be a divine Messiah. This Messiah concept was consistent with views that were circulating in the first century C.E. The earliest followers of Yeshua were able to make the claims they did because their views were firmly rooted in Jewish soil. Although this understanding within Judaism would not last long, there was a period in time when belief in a divine Messiah was indeed Jewish.

JOSHUA BRUMBACH is the Assistant Director of the newly established David Harold Stern Center for Messianic Jewish Learning and Life, and the Assistant Rabbi of Beth Emunah Messianic Synagogue—both in the Los Angeles area. He holds a degree in Ancient Near Eastern Civilizations and Biblical Studies from UCLA, and is currently completing graduate work in Jewish Studies at Messianic Jewish Theological Institute.

Jackson-McCabe, Matt, ed. *Jewish Christianity Reconsidered: Rethinking Ancient Groups and Texts*. Minneapolis: Fortress Press, 2007.

reviewed by ISAAC W. OLIVER

Scholars have made considerable progress since the nineteenth and early twentieth centuries, when specialists in ancient Judaism and early Christianity, such as Emil Schürer, referred to the Judaism of Jesus' time as *Spätjudentum* ("Late Judaism").[1] The use of this term reflected the common Christian belief that ancient Judaism, as a religion consumed by decadence, had been rightly replaced by its superior, shinier Christian peer. For too long, the reading of the New Testament was entirely divorced from its Jewish context, and many of its ancient authors, especially Paul, were viewed as the first great Christian (and consequently non-Jewish) theologians of the Church.

However, certain events proved decisive in transforming this Christian anti-Jewish rhetoric into a favorable formulation of Judaism. The discovery of the Dead Sea Scrolls, written during the Second Temple period—the new term now used as a replacement for the inadequate and admittedly biased term "inter-testamental Judaism"—informed Christian and Jewish scholars alike of the great diversity and vitality of Judaism in antiquity. In addition, the terrible events of the Holocaust as well as the establishment of a modern Jewish State shook the foundations of Christian supersessionism, forcing Christian scholars to reassess their theological and historical presuppositions about Judaism. The New Testament was finally viewed again within its Jewish matrix. Instead of talking of Jesus, Paul, and Peter as the first Christians, these characters were now reclaimed as Jewish figures who shared ideas and practices common to the diverse world of Second Temple Judaism.

Although the books and main protagonists of the New Testament are now included by mainstream scholarship within the Jewish stock, what elements, if any, are distinctive and may qualify as "Christian"? Such are the current challenges for scholars seeking to re-define the entities of "Christianity" and "Judaism," and the many social religious groups lying in-between and beyond these two poles of the spectrum. This project becomes particularly acute when discussing the so-called

1. E.g. Emil Schürer, *Geschichte des jüdischen Volkes im Zeitalter Jesu Christi* (3d/4th ed.; Leipzig: J. C. Hinrichs, 1901–1907).

75

entity of Judeo-Christians, a group of early Christians who have been defined in various ways by scholars as "Jewish" either because of their ethnicity, allegiance to the Torah, or appropriation of some form of discourse that is identified as being particularly Jewish. These questions are now discussed in a new book edited by Matt Jackson-McCabe, *Jewish Christianity Reconsidered*. This volume coincides with the publication of another important work dealing with many similar issues edited by Oskar Skarsaune and Reidar Hvalvik.[2] Both works explore the various New Testament books that portray early followers of Jesus not simply as Christian, but also as Jewish, hence Jewish-Christian.

While some may entirely discard the utility of defining an ancient entity as "Jewish-Christian," since, in principle, all of early Christianity could be viewed as Jewish, McCabe and many of the contributors of his book still believe that such a categorization proves useful, since its ambiguity forces modern thinkers to reassess their conceptualization of Christianity and Judaism. McCabe provides his own introductory article on the history of research of Jewish-Christianity, underlying the problems attached to this label and describing the different presuppositions held by scholars who have approached the topic. Many will find this article extremely helpful for providing a broad, clear discussion on the various nuanced attempts made by scholars in defining Jewish Christianity.

Earlier scholarship tended to reduce the significance of ancient Judeo-Christians by confining their existence to heretical groups that were either ethnically Jewish and/or attached to Torah observance. More recent research has gradually moved away from such assumptions and developed new positions and vocabulary in an attempt to redefine this ambiguous category. The various terms, with different meanings depending on the scholar who coined them, are listed in McCabe's chapter and include among others: "Semitic Christianity," "Judaic Christianity," "Judaistic Christianity," "Hebrew Christianity," "Hebraic Christianity," and more recently "Christian Judaism." This diverse taxonomy reflects the difficulty scholars have had in classifying this ambiguous brand of early Christians. Of course, we should remember that this scholarly jargon is entirely artificial and modern. None of the early Jewish followers of Jesus would have identified themselves as "Jewish-Christian," since the entities of Christianity and (rabbinic) Judaism were still in the making. Nevertheless, McCabe and some of his colleagues find it useful to talk of such categories in order to make better sense of the complex and diverse worlds in which these early followers of Jesus lived. Certain readers who are familiar with

2. Oskar Skarsaune and Reidar Hvalvik, *Jewish Believers in Jesus: The Early Centuries* (Peabody, Mass: Hendrickson Publishers, 2007).

contemporary Jewish-Christian movements will find this semantic discussion particularly interesting, as it seems to parallel in some ways the equally puzzling and diverse worlds of modern Messianic Jews, Hebrew Christians, Hebrew Catholics, Hebrew/Jewish Adventists, and so on.

Besides McCabe's very helpful article on the history of research and the different morphologies of Jewish Christianity, other chapters of this book written by various authors are concerned with either specific books or groups of early Christians and their relation to the rubric of "Jewish Christianity." Here a variety of interpretations emerge depending on the scholar and ancient literature involved. Perhaps, the most significant and provocative position is formulated by John W. Marshall's article, "John's Jewish (Christian?) Apocalypse."[3] Marshall is correct in disagreeing with Adela Yarbo Collins, who described the author of the Book of Revelation as alienated from the Judaism of his time.[4] More significantly, Marshall argues that the epithet "Jewish-Christian" is inappropriate for understanding the value of Revelation as a thoroughly Jewish writing. Marshall prefers to qualify Revelation as simply Jewish in order to highlight its author's solidarity and identification with Judaism. Marshall's corrective, in my opinion, is persuasive and convincing. When read in this light, Marshall interprets verses such as Rev 2:9 ("those who say they are Jews but are not, but are a synagogue of Satan") not as a statement demarcating Christians from other Jews, but rather as an appropriation by the author of Revelation of the term "Jew" as one belonging to him.[5] The author of Revelation identified himself with other Jews and chose to direct his invective against non-Jews as well as the Roman Empire, which he saw as responsible for the crucifixion of Jesus and the destruction of Jerusalem.[6]

Equally interesting is Jonathan Draper's article, "The Holy Vine of David Made Known to the Gentiles through God's Servant Jesus: "Christian Judaism" in the *Didache*."[7] Draper places the *Didache* within the category of "Christian Judaism," and believes that the admonition in *Didache* 6:2–3 ("For if you can bear the entire

---

3. John W. Marshall, "John's Jewish (Christian?) Apocalypse," in *Jewish Christianity Reconsidered: Rethinking Ancient Groups and Texts* (ed. Matt Jackson-McCabe; Minneapolis: Fortress Press, 2007), 233–56.

4. Adela Yarbo Collins, *Crisis and Catharsis: The Power of the Apocalypse* (Philadelphia: Westminster, 1984).

5. John W. Marshall, "John's Jewish (Christian?) Apocalypse," 251–52.

6. Ibid., 253–55.

7. Jonathan Draper, "The Holy Vine of David Made Known to the Gentiles through God's Servant Jesus: 'Christian Judaism' in the *Didache*," in *Jewish Christianity Reconsidered: Rethinking Ancient Groups and Texts*, 257–83.

yoke of the Lord, you will be perfect; but if you cannot, do as much as you can. And concerning food, bear what you can . . . .") was addressed to Gentile converts. Accordingly, the community of the *Didache*, in a similar fashion to the council of Jerusalem as described in Acts 15, decided not to impose upon non-Jewish Christians the obligation to observe the Torah in its entirety, but did encourage gradual adoption of Mosaic precepts, which could have even included circumcision.[8] In contrast to certain scholars, Draper rightly disagrees with qualifying the community of the *Didache* as having separated from Judaism, positioning it instead within the broad and diverse world of the Jewish Diaspora.[9] Draper concludes that the *Didache* represents the first adaptation of the followers of Jesus to the world of Diaspora Judaism and to the Gentiles who wished to associate themselves with them, not requiring non-Jews to practice circumcision in order to fellowship with them but hoping for the eschatological age when Gentiles would completely submit themselves to the yoke of the Torah.[10]

Along similar lines of reasoning, Warren Carter's article "Matthew's Gospel: Jewish Christianity, Christian Judaism, or Neither?"[11] debates whether Matthew's Gospel should be viewed as a "Christian-Jewish" or a "Jewish-Christian" document. Warren first refers to Anthony J. Saldarini, who viewed Matthew's Gospel as addressing a Christian-Jewish community and representing a Christian form of Judaism.[12] Saldarini believed that the Matthean comments on Law, Messiah, and Jewish authorities stemmed from someone inside the Jewish community and were representative of first-century Judaism. Saldarini went as far as taking Matthew's silence on circumcision as evidence for the Gospel's support for such a practice among Gentile converts.[13]

Carter then turns to Hagner who has argued more recently that Matthew crafted a Jewish form of Christianity instead of a "Christian Judaism" (contra Saldarini).

8. Ibid., 260–63.

9. Ibid., 258.

10. Ibid., 281–82.

11. Warren Carter, "Matthew's Gospel: Jewish Christianity, Christian Judaism, or Neither?" in *Jewish Christianity Reconsidered: Rethinking Ancient Groups and Texts*, 155–79.

12. Anthony J. Saldarini argued for the former category in his book *Matthew's Christian-Jewish Community* (Chicago Studies in the History of Judaism; Chicago and London: University of Chicago Press, 1994). More recently, Donald Hagner has promoted the latter category in "Matthew: Christian Judaism or Jewish Christianity?" in *The Face of New Testament Studies: A Survey of Recent Research* (ed. S. McKnight and G. Osborne; Grand Rapids: Baker Academic, 2004), 263–82.

13. Saldarini, *Matthew's Christian-Jewish Community*, 156–60.

Hagner's thesis, however, is based on certain theological assumptions, which in my opinion are no longer adequate. As noted by Carter, Hagner overemphasizes the supposed uniqueness and newness of the Gospel of Matthew in order to argue that Matthew's community had been dislocated from first century Judaism. But the study of early Christianity within its Jewish context reveals how much the first Christians shared common ideas and practices with their fellow Jews. It is no longer possible to aggrandize the novelty of early Christianity, especially when Jesus and his movement are studied within history and placed in their proper Jewish sphere. Thus, Carter sides with Saldarini's taxonomy, preferring to classify Matthew as part of Christian Judaism rather than representing a new form of Jewish Christianity.

Nevertheless, Carter highlights the limitations of such a definition, since it only signals one facet of the Gospel of Matthew (its interaction with Judaism) and overlooks other aspects that the author of Matthew was confronted by, namely, Roman imperialism. According to Carter, the ways in which the Gospel of Matthew negotiated with life under Roman imperial rule is a question that has been highly neglected by scholarship. Analyzing different Jewish and non-Jewish responses to Roman power is a promising field for further research.

While Hagner, Marshall, and Draper represent the current trend, which emphasizes early Christianity's inclusion within its Jewish environment, Raimo Hakola, on the other hand, seems to go against the swing of the pendulum by underlining the impropriety of classifying the Gospel of John as Jewish-Christian. In "The Johannine Community as Jewish Christians? Some Problems in Current Scholarly Consensus,"[14] Hakola relates how mainstream scholarship at the end of the nineteenth and beginning of the twentieth century saw behind the Gospel of John a community that had drifted away from its Jewish roots. Johannine features such as its christology, determinism, and dualism were understood as being part of the generalizing rubric of "Hellenism." John was viewed by some as reflecting a time when the earlier conflicts between Hellenistic Christians and Jewish Christians were left behind and the separation of Christianity from Judaism had been completed. But with the discovery of the Dead Sea Scrolls, scholars reaffirmed the Jewishness of the fourth canonical Gospel. Certain features, such as John's dualism, could now be compared with the dualism of the sectarian Qumranites (e.g., the Community Rule).

---

14. Raimo Hakola, "The Johannine Community as Jewish Christians? Some Problems in Current Scholarly Consensus," in *Jewish Christianity Reconsidered: Rethinking Ancient Groups and Texts*, 181–201.

Nevertheless, Hakola believes that it is improper to apply the epithet "Jewish-Christian" to the Johannine community, unless this term is confined to its ethnic-ideological dimension. At the praxis level (Torah observance), however, the Johannine community does not fit well within the Jewish-Christian rubric, since, according to Hakola, Jesus is portrayed in John as above the Law and as superior to Moses.[15] Hakola also discards interpreting the Johannine community as a group persecuted by the leading Jewish authorities (often identified with the early rabbis), claiming that no evidence exists for such synagogue-organized persecutions, and that other theological and religious developments must be taken into account in explaining the Johaninne community's estrangement from the rest of Judaism.[16] While we may not be totally dissuaded from identifying John's Gospel as Jewish-Christian in its widest sense, Hakola's remarks remind us of the complicated and ambivalent relationship which existed between the Johannine community and its Jewish surroundings.

The remaining articles deal with various Jewish-Christian groups (e.g., Ebionites and Nazarenes) or other early Christian books (e.g., the Letter of James, Pseudo-Clementine literature, and the Q document). In sum, then, this book provides the reader with a useful introduction to many of the main issues related to the study of Jewish Christianity. While a unified, cohesive treatment written by one scholar on this important topic is greatly desired, the reader, in the meantime, will have to learn the various methods used by different scholars who wrestle with this subject. McCabe's edition, then, probably provides the best starting point for such an inquiry, since it is intentionally written with a broad audience in mind, avoiding excessive scholarly technicalities, and presenting its content in a clear and accessible way. As such, this book will prove useful for students of the university at all levels and even for specialists of ancient Judaism and Christianity. The general educated reader, interested in Judaism and Christianity, will also be able to listen in and enjoy the different discussions. Moreover, the readers of this journal will especially find this book intriguing as it addresses issues that in certain ways are reminiscent of the contemporary Jewish-Christian (and/or Messianic) movements.

ISAAC W. OLIVER is a Ph.D. student in Judaism and Christianity in the Graeco-Roman World at the University of Michigan. Isaac completed his B.A. and M.A. in Religion at Andrews University, MI.

15. Ibid., 186–92.

16. Ibid., 185.

Lustiger, Jean-Marie Cardinal. *The Promise*. Grand Rapids: Eerdmans, 2007.

reviewed by STUART DAUERMANN

Jean-Marie Cardinal Lustiger (1926–2007), a child of Polish-born secularized Jewish parents, was raised in Paris, and, with his family, fled to the south of France (Orléans) during WW II. Tragically, his mother returned to Paris to take care of business affairs, was betrayed by her maid and deported to Auschwitz where she was murdered. Lustiger came across a Protestant Bible as a young adolescent, and, in August of his 14th year, became a convert, a conversion his father unsuccessfully sought to have reversed. His sister also converted. Lustiger and his father were reconciled in the 1970s, and the then Bishop Lustiger made arrangements for the Jewish funeral of his father. He was Archbishop Emeritus of Paris and throughout his life stood faithfully as a witness to Jewish suffering, the elect status of the Jewish people, and to Christ, the crucified. In religiously liberal France, he was known as an excellent communicator and, like close friend John Paul II, modern in his style and traditional in his convictions. He was considered by some to be a logical successor to John Paul, but he demurred for reasons of health.

This compilation brings together a collection of meditations on the Gospel of Matthew delivered to a group of French contemplative nuns, supplemented by a few brief addresses delivered in the 1990s to various Jewish audiences. Throughout, Lustiger demonstrates an unflinching and consistent conviction that Israel is the elect people of God and that Jesus is first and foremost their Savior and Redeemer. Furthermore, without exception, he refers to Gentiles, even Gentile Christians as "pagans," underscoring that Christian access to the grace of God is always via God's prior and continuing mercy to Israel. In this book, he explores the ways in which both Israel and the Church need each other, the contours of their respective and collective missions, and ways the attitudes of each community toward the other must change if they are to fulfill their destiny and responsibility to God and to humankind.

In chapter one, "Jesus and the Law," he argues against seeing Jews and their law as superseded by another code and another people. Jesus is presented as exemplifying and ratifying Torah obedience. God is seen as enabling Yeshua-believers to walk in the obedience of Messiah, patterned after the Law, and facilitated by the Spirit.

In chapter two, "The Ten Words," he shows how God himself exemplifies the righteous requirements of the Ten Words.

In chapter three, "Prophecy Concerning the Life of Jesus," he examines the Matthean nativity story and the corporate solidarity of Jesus and Israel.

In chapter four, "Prophecy of the Life of the Disciples of Jesus," he continues by considering the second chapter of Matthew, seeing it as foreshadowing the mission of Messiah, the Church and the final judgment as well as the unity between those who suffer for the Kingdom of God (including faithful Israel), and the kingdom of God and Messiah. Matthew 2 also underlies chapter five, "The Passion of Christ Throughout History," in which he considers how the Church rejects Messiah whenever it rejects or persecutes Israel, highlighting the solidarity between the sufferings of Israel and those of Messiah.

In chapter six, "In Him, All God's Promises Are Fulfilled," he demonstrates how in Yeshua, the Kingdom of God is a present reality among us but in a secret form, not yet fully and triumphantly manifest. Through the gift of the Spirit, Yeshua's eschatological foreshadowing of Israel's blessed future is communicated to us. Our foretaste of the age to come is a foretaste of Israel's prophetic destiny—obedience to Torah, fullness of the Spirit, resurrection of the dead, and regathering of God's people—all signs borrowed from Ezekiel 36–37.

In chapter seven, "The Hope of Israel," Lustiger examines the third chapter of Matthew, again countering supersessionism by presenting Yeshua the Messiah as Israel's hope. The Hebrew Bible is not invalidated by his coming but extended to the pagans through the New Covenant and Messiah, and this is a grace immersed in sufferings now, with glories to follow. We live between the already and the not yet, just as Yeshua was not yet glorified. The passion of Messiah reveals both the measure of our sin and the scope of our forgiveness; we could not bear the knowledge of our sin otherwise. We can then go on in the Holy Spirit, willing to suffer for his name's sake.

In chapter eight, "Christ's Passion Reveals the Sin of All," he explores the mystery of Messiah: Why was it "necessary" that the Messiah had to die? In the account of Messiah's passion we see representatives of every class of humankind, all demonstrated to be in need of the fruits of his passion. In Messiah, we see the character and depth of our sin. Through this same passion, we are enabled to live a new life in union with Messiah through his outpoured Spirit.

In chapter nine, "Jesus Crucified, the Messiah of Israel: Salvation for All," he shows how the salvation Christian pagans receive is a participation in the election of

Israel. For both Israel and the Church this should result in holy living. Israel and the Church are meant to have a reciprocal relationship.

In chapter ten, "Access Through Christ to All the Riches of Israel," he considers the riches accessible to the pagan nations through the cross of Messiah. Among these he names access to Israel's history, her Law, her Scripture, her prayer life and festivals, her land, the Kingdom of God, the redemption and repentance. It seems that for Lustiger, these are already the possession of Israel apart from explicit Yeshua-faith.

In chapter eleven, "Facing Israel—The Nations' Examination of Conscience," he shows how the Church and the nations are responsible for anti-Semitism and must repent by reaffirming the unique and elect status of Israel, while allowing Israel to be who she is before God. Perhaps then the wound between Israel and the Church will begin to heal. Lustiger hopes for the rebirth of what was lost in the early centuries, a church from among the circumcision.

The final four small chapters consist of brief addresses given to Jewish audiences. In chapter twelve, "Israel and the Gentiles," he speaks of how Israel must transcend merely national concerns because its election is not for itself alone. In chapter thirteen, "From Jules Isaac to John Paul II," he examines the contribution of the latter, the heroic reopening of dialogue after 2000 years, post-Auschwitz, the recovery of memory which Auschwitz sought to obliterate, the need for Christians and Jews to continue to find each other and their reciprocal destinies across the table of the Bible, which neither of them ultimately defines, but which defines them both.

In chapter fourteen, "What Can Jews and Christians Hope for When They Meet?," he shows how Jews remain "other" and "strangers" in the midst of the earth, yet may discover deep commonality with Christians. Through dialogue, both Jews and Christians may and should come to better understand themselves in ways they could not otherwise access. This renewed dialogue promises an unforeseen and salutary fecundity.

In chapter fifteen, "What Do Christian-Jewish Encounters Mean as Civilizations Clash?," he explores the interwoven/converging destines of Israel and the Church through considering five questions: (1) What do Jews and Christians have in common that may justify their getting closer to each other, and becoming allies?; (2) As Jews and Christians acknowledge what they have in common, will their respective characteristics and identities be threatened by such companionship?; (3) Does this common principle mean anything for humankind as a whole?; (4) Do both Jews and Christians become better able, when they get together, to carry out their specific mission with regard to the rest of humankind?; and finally (5) If such caring for the world does not reflect any ambition to conquer or dominate, how can this universalism express itself completely? Lustiger handles these enormous questions with seemingly effortless grace. He states clearly that God's call upon Jews and Christians precludes their failing to dialogue and work together. The world needs Jews and Christians to do this, and God commands it.

The book spans nearly thirty years of the author's life while exhibiting unwavering unity. What strikes me most is his unabashed confidence in the Election of Israel, and how the Church's destiny is derivative from, and contingent upon, Israel inheriting what the Father promised. This she does through God's grace in Yeshua.

I needed to step back and ponder this book for quite some time. At first blush, he seems to accord to Israel more of a free pass than seems warranted. However, before rejecting his perspective, one must note that he sees Yeshua from within Jewish space, rather than as an outside option that Israel must either accept or reject. Yeshua remains for Lustiger ever and always the Messiah of Israel and only therefore the Savior of the nations. I am challenged to examine my communal location as I contemplate the mystery of Israel and of God's grace in Messiah, for so much hangs upon that social location. This is a small book requiring of all of us a big look, offering a window into a mind and soul much larger than most.

STUART DAUERMANN (Ph.D., Fuller Theological Seminary) is Senior Scholar at Messianic Jewish Theological Institute and President of Hashivenu, a Messianic Jewish think-tank. He serves as Rabbi of Ahavat Zion Messianic Synagogue in Beverly Hills, CA.

Kaminskky, Joel S. *Yet I Loved Jacob: Reclaiming the Biblical Concept of Election.* Nashville: Abingdon Press, 2007.

reviewed by STUART DAUERMANN

Joel Kaminsky is Director of the Program in Jewish Studies at Smith College in Northampton, Massachusetts. He teaches courses on the Hebrew Bible and on ancient Jewish Religion and Literature.

Kaminsky believes that the Christian and Jewish communities stand to learn something new about each other and themselves by seeing Scripture through each other's eyes, and through separately and together revisiting the Bible as it illumines the foundations and development of election, a doctrine neither community can afford to ignore or jettison. As he demonstrates in the book's introduction, the modern aversion to election is due to the twin legacies of Enlightenment— preference for the universal over the particular and the legacy of supersessionism. Unlike other books on election that begin with word studies, his work engages the text of Scripture itself, taking a canonical approach, with special attention given to narrative nuance and intertextuality.

In Part 1 (chapters one to four), he examines the four patriarchal sibling rivalry stories that lay a seedbed for the Bible's doctrine of election. In chapter one, the case of Cain and Abel, we see one of four stories of God preferring the younger to the elder, and of the younger going into exile. God's choices are mysterious. He chooses the elect not for their benefit alone; the non-elect are also blessed, but must learn not to resent the elect who are God's chosen and a means of God's blessing them. The story of Cain and Abel, non-elect and elect siblings, is embryonic of what will be more fully developed throughout Genesis, culminating in the Joseph saga.

The pattern continues in chapter two, with Ishmael and Isaac (and Hagar and Sarah) whose family/sibling rivalry stories demonstrate how human agency can impede divine intent. Yet, in Ishmael, we see the blessedness of the non-elect, a major theme in Kaminsky's treatment.

In chapter three, on Jacob and Esau, he explores the ambiguities inherent in God's election, especially the question of whether human choices, even devious choices, are necessary to or expeditious of the Divine program. Also covered are the themes of reconciliation between the chosen and the non-chosen siblings, and an excellent discussion of the varieties of reconciliation, and how these do not require a return to a *status quo ante*.

In chapter four, on Joseph, he examines the issue of the suffering of the elect who are tested, and, if they endure the test, purified by their suffering, through which they have the opportunity to glorify God.

In chapter five, Kaminsky looks at the interrelationship between promise, covenant, and commandment. He views covenants as "formalizations of promises made to Israel's ancestors as well as of Israel's self understanding that they are God's chosen people" (p. 84). For Kaminsky, the full scope and meaning of Israel's calling is not entirely spelled out in Scripture, nor can that calling be collapsed into service, as much Christian theologizing does. This chapter explores types of covenants (human/human; divine/human; conditional/unconditional), and demonstrates that the categories conditional/unconditional are not absolute.

In chapter six, he examines how notions of law and holiness, as enumerated in Leviticus and Deuteronomy, relate to election. For Kaminsky, these works highlight different facets of holiness.

In his introduction to chapters seven and eight, he provides an overview concerning "Israel and the Other," surveying misguided negative opinions that postulate the Hebrew Bible's stance on the matter, and its moral implications, as being fascist and genocidal. Kaminsky shows how a close reading of the text reveals that Israel was not called to exterminate all who are termed "other," but rather only the Amalekites, Canaanites, and to some extent, Midianites. There was a *modus vivendi* for the other nations surrounding Israel. Many fail to note that the Hebrew Bible considers nations as elect, non-elect, or anti-elect. The elect nation is Israel, the non-elect nations are blessed with Israel and because of Israel, and only the anti-elect, who are enemies of Israel and of her God, face perdition and exclusion from blessedness. Scholars who reject the doctrine of Israel's election on moral grounds generally misunderstand the text and demonstrate ignorance of these distinctions.

In chapter seven, Kaminsky examines the anti-elect as those who are enemies of God and of his people and thus are targeted for destruction. He says that although these passages remain problematic, those who equate the Hebrew and Nazi positions and who condemn these passages outright, fail to consider how the passages deserve a more sympathetic reading. Even if the more sympathetic reading fails to erase all the troubling aspects of the texts, the doctrine of election should not be jettisoned. As he notes, later Jewish tradition formulated a number of ways to mitigate the hard edges of the theology of the anti-elect. The first is to attempt to justify God's delay in wiping out the Canaanites/Amalekites, while acknowledging their deep depravity and evil. The second way is to posit that only the determinedly wicked were slain (in the Canaanite campaign) after being given ample opportunity to accept terms of peace. The third way is to spiritualize annihilation by removing evil from the world and/or resisting evil impulses.

In chapter eight, "The Non-Elect in the Hebrew Bible," Kaminsky reminds his readers that the Hebrew Bible is often surprisingly positive toward the non-Israelite, both individuals and groups, and that some groups whom one would imagine receiving harsh treatment are in fact slated for favor (as is the case for Egypt). This becomes especially explicit in narrative passages, so that foreign figures are treated with respect (e.g., Melchizedek, the Pharaoh of Joseph's day, Jael, the wife of Heber the Kenite, Hiram, king of Tyre, the Queen of Sheba, the widow of Zarephath, Cyrus, King of Persia, and the non-Israelite sailors in Jonah's boat). Sometimes foreign groups are merged with the people of Israel e.g., (Rahab and her family, Reuel/Hobab/Jethro, and Moses' father in law). In treating the assimilation of foreigners, Kaminsky references Shaye Cohen who argues that Judaism was probably not even considered a religion until the Hellenistic period. Before then, it was an ethnic and tribal identification. "It is more accurate to speak of individuals or groups attaching themselves to God or God's people rather than the term 'conversion' and all that it implies" (p. 126).

In chapter nine, "Prophecy and Election," he explores further how modern authors consistently read their own concerns and presuppositions into the text. For example, scholars such as Walter Brueggemann and John Collins read Amos 9:7 as stating that Israel is no longer a unique nation, but just one like the others. Kaminsky states that the harsh language refers not to God suspending Israel's covenant identity but rather to his calling Israel back to covenant faithfulness.

In his section on "The Purpose of Election: Instrumental or Intrinsic," Kaminsky begins by discussing how supersessionism often underlies positions that view Israel's election as purely instrumental. The standard argument is that Israel failed, Messiah succeeded, and the role of Israel passed to the Church. In Isaiah, the Servant Songs are especially the locus for this debate. Contrary to this, Kaminsky states that:

> it is quite unlikely that these eschatologically charged texts found in 2nd Isaiah ever conceived of extending Israel's elect status to the other nations of the world. . . . In fact, it is theologically incoherent that the very prophet who most stresses God's deep, unbreakable love for his unique people would call on them to dissolve their uniqueness by extending their elect

> status to everyone in the world. Election by definition requires that dis-
> tinctions be maintained between God's people and those not elected. . . .
> The Hebrew Bible resists reducing the meaning of Israel's special election
> to a matter of divine service (Deut 9:4–7; Jer 31:1–20). If one links election
> too strongly to service, it is impossible to understand why God restores
> Israel from exile. The answer, of course, is that in spite of Israel's failures,
> she remains beloved by God (p. 154).

And of course, this is what we learn in Romans 11:28–29.

It is in his discussion of the relationship between Second Isaiah, the Servant Songs, and the Joseph story that things really begin to crackle with electric relevance for the Messianic Jewish context. In the servant passages and the Joseph narrative, there are three basic categories of people: the elect of the elect who receive special attention within each text, those belonging to the larger elect group but not specially chosen, and the other nations of the world. In the Joseph story, the elect of the elect is, of course, Joseph himself, while in Isaiah it is the Israelite person or group associated with the servant language [for the Messianic Jewish community, the Messiah himself and the Remnant of Israel]. In both texts, the especially elect brings about reconciliation between the especially elect one and the larger group as a whole. Thus, the bulk of the Joseph story focuses on how the divided sons of Israel are reunited again in a way that overcomes many of the family troubles that led to the original rift and gives theological meaning to Joseph's suffering (Gen 45:5–8). Kaminsky avers that, while the image of the servant is notoriously difficult to pin down firmly, it is fair to say that there are indeed places in the latter chapters of Isaiah in which the servant person or group functions as the specially elect who brings about renewed national unity (Isa 42:6–7; 49:5) in a way that gives theological meaning to the suffering of the elect. Certainly, the suffering of this elect person or group brings about a national rejuvenation. Finally, in the Joseph story, while the focus is more immediately on Jacob's extended family, the result is that Joseph, working under a benign Pharaoh, preserves the whole world and thus brings God's blessing to the nations (Gen 41:57). Similarly, in Isaiah while the restoration of Israel as a people is the focus of the text, the specially elect, working under the benign Cyrus, foresee that the ultimate goal will be the recognition of God's sovereignty throughout the world, which will result in a renewed cosmos in which God's blessing will become fully manifest to the benefit of all (p. 157).

Extrapolating from Kaminsky's model, I suggest that there are at least six postures the Church should take in relationship to the Jewish people:

1. *Respect for Israel's unique elect status.* Kaminsky shows how Israel's election is not simply for service, but out of the exercise of God's freedom and his love for the seed of Jacob.

2. *Acknowledgement of dependence.* The Church has no relationship with God independent of Israel. Paul is at pains to emphasize this point in Romans 11. Many in the Church have nonetheless forgotten, disparaged, or disputed this. This is the legacy of supersessonism whereby the Church does not join with Israel but rather replaces her.

3. *Gratitude to God.* Failure of acknowledgement insults the people of Israel, while ingratitude insults God.

4. *Co-laboring.* The Church should seek every opportunity to work with the seed of Jacob and to understand her own vocation through respecting and understanding that of Israel.

5. *Anticipation.* Seeing her own identity rooted in that of Israel, the Church should also anticipate a consummation in which both Israel and the Church are involved, indeed, one in which the Church has become part of the commonwealth of Israel, with her destiny inseparably intertwined with that of Israel.

6. *An attitude of humility in the presence of gradually unfolding mystery.* Paul speaks of mystery with respect to the outworking of God's purposes concerning Israel and the Church. He himself struggles to understand what God is doing, demonstrating awe, respect and humility before the gradually unfolding mystery. The Church should do no less.

In chapter ten, Kaminsky examines "Election in Psalms and the Wisdom Literature," finding in these sources echoes of the world view explored in Israel's foundational election texts, the sibling narratives of Genesis and the rest of Torah.

In chapter eleven, "New Testament and Rabbinic Views of Election," he begins by affirming that particularistic election is as much a Christian category as a Jewish one and that the New Covenant appropriates this Jewish category and related language for its own use (as in 1 Peter 2:9–10; cf. Exod 19:5–6). It is especially fascinating that he sees the gospel story as a form of sibling rivalry story. He writes,

> The master narrative of the New Testament—the passion, death, and res-
> urrection of Jesus—is itself a re-presentation of the central motif of the
> sibling rivalry stories from Genesis: the death and resurrection of the
> beloved son. Thus, the church saw Jesus, and by association those who
> believed in him, as the chosen son who was persecuted and ultimately
> exalted (p. 171).

This reading of the Joseph story can be easily related to a Messianic Jewish perspective. He came unto his own, and his own received him not. In fact, his brothers killed
him by the hands of others. God brought him back, and he will be proven to be the
best friend the children of Israel ever had.

Kaminsky represents Judaism as, in the main, following the lead of the Hebrew
Bible, viewing the non-elect as still candidates for God's blessing. He contrasts this
with Christianity, which, in the main, thinks in binary categories of elect/saved vs.
non-elect/lost. For Christianity, unlike the Hebrew Bible, there is no difference in
soteriological status between the anti-elect and the non-elect. While Christianity is
more open to others as potential converts, it is less able than Judaism to receive the
"other" as "other".

In his section "Grace and Works in Judaism and Christianity," Kaminsky dis-
misses as simplistic and inaccurate generalizations portraying Christianity as a religion of faith apart from works, and Judaism as a religion of works as contrasted with
faith. He shows that it is unhelpful and inaccurate to view Judaism through Christian
categories. Unlike many forms of Christianity, Judaism does not view grace and law
to be antithetical, viewing the giving of the law as a magnificent act of grace.

Kaminsky lends credence to the post-supersessionist perspective I favor, as he
assumes that both the Christian and Jewish communities must hear the voice of the
other in order not only to critique and expand their own self-understanding as well
as learn about each other, but also that together they might be better able to discern
the new things that God is doing that would not otherwise be anticipated, understood, or welcomed. Only by listening to each other will we develop ears to hear what
God is saying to us separately and together at this time. Those who deafen their ears
to the voice of their brother, even their estranged brother, cannot expect to rightly
hear the voice of God. This book is crucial for the Messianic Jewish movement as a
resource informing a deep repudiation of supersessionism and as a call to reclaim
the elect status which belongs to the seed of Jacob because of God's love toward
them, a love proceeding not out of their deserving but out of his own freedom.

The book also challenges us to recognize how some hard-line binary categories may not be really "either/or" but rather "both/and." Kaminsky's discussion underscores that the non-elect are not necessarily lost under God's judgment but may in fact be blessed with the elect. The lost/judged are rather "the wicked (who) will be turned to Sheol, all the nations that forget God" (Ps 9:18). Also of use is his discussion of how the elect of the elect bring blessing to the elect—which in New Covenant terms reminds us of what so many forget: that the Remnant of Israel are the guarantors and means of blessing to the rest of Israel, and thereby to the non-elect—the other nations. This book is crucial to the formation of a Messianic Jewish theology, missiology, and ecclesiology. We have yet to catch up to the level of Kaminsky's thought.

Stuart Dauermann (Ph.D., Fuller Theological Seminary) is Senior Scholar at Messianic Jewish Theological Institute and President of Hashivenu, a Messianic Jewish think-tank. He serves as Rabbi of Ahavat Zion Messianic Synagogue in Beverly Hills, CA.